Contents

Introduction 1
A Law is Passed: The Lord Advocate's Speech 5
Something Must Be Done 17
The New Poorhouse 29
Running the Poorhouse 59
The Inmates 95
Medical Care 115
In Court 133
The Catholic Priest's Cab Fare 147
Eternal Damnation 153
The Ultramontane Miss Weir 175
Some Notable Events at the Poorhouse 185
Epilogue: The Poorhouse Poet 191
Appendix: The Burning of the Ship 'Kent' by William McGonagall .. 203
List of Illustrations 206

The Edinburgh City Poorhouse monogram on the main staircase.

Introduction

In 1856, 'A History of the Scotch Poor Law in connexion with the condition of the people' by Sir George Nicholls records:

By a Parliament held at Edinburgh in 1449, it was ordained *"for the away putting of sornares[1], overlyars[2] and masterful beggars, that all sheriffs, barons, aldermen, and bailies, as well within burgh as without, shall take inquisitions of such persons at each court that they hold, and if any such be found, that they shall be imprisoned at the King's will, and their horses, hounds and other goods be escheated[3]. And also, that the Sheriffs and other officers inquire at each court if there be any that follow the profession of fools, that are not bardis[4], or sick like rinners about[5]. And if any such be found, they are to be imprisoned or put in irons for their trespass, as long as they have any goods of their own to live upon. And if they have nothing to live upon, their ears are to be nailed to the trone (public weighing machine), or to any other tree, and then cut off, and themselves banished the country. And if they return again, they are to be hanged".*

Society has always struggled with looking after the poor, but it is a relief we've come a long way since 1449.

When we moved into an apartment in a beautiful building on a hill in the leafy district of Craiglockhart, not three miles from Edinburgh city centre, I was naturally inquisitive about its history, it having been converted from an old folks' home to residential accommodation in the 1980s. Some background research established it had been the main administrative block for the Edinburgh City Poorhouse, opened in 1870. Beside us, a number of equally imposing, if somewhat austere, Victorian blocks in a line from East to West were married

---

1   Sornare -Scots - A person who exacts free quarters and provisions by means of threats or force as a livelihood
2   Overlyar – Scots - One who quarters himself upon another
3   Escheated – Given to the Crown
4   Bardis – Scots -A vagabond. It also meant a strolling minstrel or poet. The origin of 'Bard' e.g. Shakespeare
5   Rinners about – Scots - Fugitives

with sympathetically designed modern apartment blocks. I was told that our garage, in a long stone-built row, had once been the Poorhouse mortuary. Once the rolling countryside to the south of the city, the area had been the site of a large number of Victorian public building projects; to the north of us, the huge Craighouse Asylum, opened in 1894, to the south, the City Hospital, initially built as a fever hospital (with another mortuary nearby) opened in 1903, and to the west, the Craiglockhart Hydropathic, opened in 1880, best known as a military hospital in WW1, whose patients included Wilfred Owen and Siegfried Sassoon.

Like many, I had not much knowledge of how poorhouses operated beyond *Oliver Twist*, but I had established my Great Great Grandmother had died, after three marriages and numerous children, in the Inveresk Combination Poorhouse in 1881 and I was curious to know more. I also discovered that my Great Grandparents were both asylum attendants in Melrose when they married in Musselburgh in 1873. Before 1872, lunatics in the Scottish Borders were treated in Musselburgh, but the 1857 Lunacy (Scotland) Act provided for a new asylum to be built at Melrose. I was pleased to learn the new asylum in Melrose was run on more enlightened lines, with inmates' welfare at heart, rather than just incarceration. I leave it to the reader to decide how much that was the case at Craiglockhart.

I have based my research mostly on the British Newspaper Archive, which holds copies of local and national newspapers, and gradually became increasingly absorbed as I read on. Victorian newspapers are an entertaining read, if rather close printed and dense, but they present a vivid portrait of life, politics, scandals, crimes, local government and the ebb and flow of society. They are opinionated, wordy, gossipy, pompous, funny, judgmental and fortunately very detailed, which has proved to be a great help in getting to know the City Poorhouse and its inhabitants. Their flowery, slightly archaic language grew on me as I went deeper; for example, one doesn't hear the term 'animadversion' much these days, sadly. This book paints a vivid picture of the late 19th Century and the early 20th at Craiglockhart Poorhouse, in the words of observers at the time, not mine.

Introduction

The Craiglockhart Poorhouse's foundations were laid in 1867. Opened in May 1870, it was managed by the City of Edinburgh Parochial Board until 1895, when it was replaced by the Edinburgh Parish Council. The Poor Laws (and Poorhouses) were replaced by the National Assistance Act in 1948. After World War II, when it was used amongst other things as a hospital for Norwegian Airmen, it became an old people's home, until redevelopment as housing in the late 1980s.

Following a look at the conditions of the times and the background to the building of the establishment, we see something of how it was managed. Fortunately, there are almost verbatim accounts of the Parochial Board meetings, which make one feel almost in the room with them, as Victorian patriarchs pontificated and thundered. The attitudes and prejudices of the times are plainly evident. There are records of events and, of course, stories of the inmates, in turn interesting and amusing, but also sad. Before the National Health Service, hospital care for the poor was very limited, and accounts of the healthcare provision in the Poorhouse paint an interesting picture of the service offered. Inevitably, the newspapers included details of court cases involving inmates, many all too predictable, but we also learn of the unfortunate downfall of one of the Governors.

No look at Scotland's history can ever get far without religious tension rearing its head. I have found three striking examples, amusing and shocking in equal part, which vividly illustrate the influence of religion on society at the time and the conflict which existed between Presbyterians, Episcopalians and Roman Catholics, which had significant impact upon those confined to the Poorhouse.

The tales end with Peter Sinclair, the Poet of the Police Court, again amusing and tragic in equal parts. The reader will be struck by many resonances in these accounts with today. While history often is a record of the great men (and occasionally the women) and major events of the time, these accounts afford us a fascinating insight into the lives of ordinary people.

Alastair MacDonald

Duncan McNeill, 1st Lord Colonsay 1793-1874.
The Lord Advocate 1845.

Chapter 1

A Law is Passed
The Lord Advocate's Speech [6]

The following speech by the Lord Advocate provides a helpful background of how the Poor Laws had operated in Scotland before 1845 and what was now proposed to reform the system.

In 1832, a Royal Commission was established to examine the Poor Laws in England, partly triggered by the concern over the cost of poor relief in Southern England. A scale of locally taxed wage supplements for rural workers (the Speenhamland System, which interestingly bore some similarity to our modern Universal Credit principle of benefits when in work, rather than only when unemployed) had caused controversy over the costs involved, but it was also criticised for suppressing wage levels.

The Commission proposed workhouse conditions should act as a deterrent, so only the neediest would consider entering. It was also thought that relief should only be available within the workhouse and that outdoor relief [7] should be abolished. *"Into such a house none will enter voluntarily; work, confinement, and discipline will deter the indolent and vicious; and nothing but extreme necessity will induce any to accept the comfort which must be obtained by the surrender of their free agency, and the sacrifice of their accustomed habits and gratifications."*

The subsequent (English) Poor Law Amendment Act of 1834 did not apply to Scotland, as it had had a separate legal system. In 1843, the 'Disruption' in the Church of Scotland, when about a third of Church of Scotland ministers broke away from the established church to form the Free Church of Scotland, significantly depleted the administration of poor relief via Kirk Sessions. It was recognised that reform was

---

6   From Hansard House of Commons 2nd of April 1845. Poor Law of Scotland - The Lord Advocate - First Reading of the Bill

7   'Outdoor relief' was welfare in the form of money, food, clothing or goods without the requirement to enter in to an institution

overdue, and a Commission of Enquiry was set up to assess the state of poor relief in Scotland, which reported in 1844 and resulted in the Poor Law (Scotland) Act of 1845.

The background to the 1845 Act is summed up in the Lord Advocate's speech during the First Reading of the Bill in the House of Commons in April of that year.

"Public attention has been for some time past a good deal directed to the state and condition of the poor in Scotland and an impression existed in some parts of that country, particularly in the great towns and some rural districts, the condition of the poor was not what it ought to be. In reference to that condition, as far back as 1838, the General Assembly of the Church of Scotland had appointed a committee to inquire and a report was made to the House of Commons, both as to the condition of the poor and to as to the law and practice of Scotland in maintaining them. In 1842 returns were moved for the House of Commons with reference to the condition of the poor in all parishes in Scotland. Those returns were printed in 1843 and a commission of enquiry was appointed. That commission pursued its labours for nearly a year, and it was impossible to speak too highly in terms of praise of those labours or the anxiety, industry and judgement evinced by the noblemen and gentlemen by whom that inquiry was conducted.

"In 1844 they made the report that was now on the table of the House. Now that report, and the evidence upon which is based, established beyond all doubt that the feeling which had previously obtained as to the condition of the poor in many parts of Scotland was not without cause. In some parts of the country, especially in the large towns, a great deal of poverty and misery existed and the application of means of relief was not what was to be wished. The same might be said of some of the rural districts. The commissioners said that the funds raised for the relief of the poor and the provision made for them out of the funds raised for the relief, is, in many parishes throughout Scotland, insufficient. The amount of relief given is frequently insufficient to provide even the commonest necessities of life. Throughout the Highland districts and in some parts of the Lowlands, also where the funds consist solely of what may be raised by the Church collections, the amount is often inconsiderable. In many of these places, the quantum of relief given is not measured by the necessities of the pauper, but by the sum which the Kirk session may happen to have in hand for distribution.

"We cannot cite a stronger instance than that of the City of Edinburgh, in which the Town Council have for years declined to increase the rate of assessment, notwithstanding applications made by the managers of the poor and representations that necessities of the poor were increasing, and the funds raised insufficient. The Lord Advocate had found himself coming to the conclusion that the condition of the poor was not what it ought to be, and some legislative interference was absolutely necessary.

"He had sometimes been congratulated in this end of the island by the absence of Poor Law in Scotland and had been met by expressions of astonishment when he said that there did exist in that country a complete system of Poor Law. To Members of the House of Commons it was known that there existed such a law and it might not be necessary to explain what the law was. The substantial provisions of the Poor Law of Scotland were contained in a Statute passed in the reign of King James VI of that Kingdom in 1579 and in two proclamations of the Privy Council in the reign of William and Mary. This was all the law that existed for any compulsory provision whatever. That statute and Proclamations might be said to constitute the Poor Law of Scotland.

"In the first place, as to the persons who were objects of the care of the Legislature, the substance of the law was that provision should be made for the infirm and impotent poor. This related to persons labouring under bodily infirmity in consequence of age or in consequence of non-age or in consequence of disease or accident. All these persons, being unable to support themselves, were the objects of the law. It was not necessary however to entitle them to be recipients of the relief that they should be totally disabled – if they were partially disabled, they might, under the law as it stood, have relief awarded to them in aid of what they could earn, so as to make up sufficient for their subsistence; but they must be either wholly or partially disabled to bring them within the provisions of the law. If they can work at all, they must work to a certain extent. That being the state of the case as to persons who were entitled to claim relief, he might now state that when such persons fell into a situation of poverty, their claim for relief lay against the parish of their settlement.

"Settlement in Scotland was gained in four ways – by birth, parentage, residence or marriage; and it was the law of Scotland that a settlement, once acquired, cannot be lost, except by acquiring another in another parish. Then as to the funds which existed for the maintenance of the poor, these consisted in the first place of contributions at the doors of the parish churches. Such contributions were made on the Sabbath at every parish church and produced no inconsiderable revenue. There were other voluntary contributions. It sometimes happened that the people of a particular district agreed to contribute on a scale which they settled for themselves; the sums were very considerable, and they were on the increase. There might also be sums "mortified" as it was called in Scotland or bequeathed for the use of the poor.

"The remaining source was the fund raised by legal assessment. In Scotland there was full power by the Statute of 1579 and the Proclamations for the parochial authorities to assess for the maintenance of the poor and that without any limits as to the amount, other than the necessities of case. That had been the law since 1579; it was the law now and, in several parishes, it was acted upon to at large extent. In towns the administration of the law fell upon the magistrates who were responsible; but practically rested with the Kirk Sessions – that was the minister and the elders of the parish. In landward parishes the administration was with the proprietors or heritors and the Kirk Sessions. It was not prescribed by statute that the relief should be in any particular form.

"The requisite was that the poor should have needful sustenation and that might be given in clothes, food, money, house-rent or in any way most advantageous to done. The amount depended on the opinion and discretion of the administrators of the fund. It can scarcely be contended that the support given to the poor should be greater than that which was earned by the labourer in full employment, supporting his family. It might happen that the poor person was denied relief – the parish might refuse to consider his case or listen to his application. If that occurred, the Sheriff of the county had full power and authority to require that the parochial authorities should meet and take the claim into consideration; there was still a remedy for the pauper by application to the Supreme Court, which had power to compel the parochial authorities.

"It would be seen that in Scotland every impotent poor person had a statutory right to relief and that in every parish there is an administrative body charged by law with the duty and armed with power of giving relief and raising funds for that purpose and the courts of law have power to compel them. It went further- the law also provided for the education of the poor; and in every parish there was a system of education supported by a parish funds and the teachers were obliged to teach the children of the poor gratuitously. It might be surprising to some to observe that, while the contemporaneous enactments were so similar in the countries of England and Scotland, practically the results of them in the progress of time had been so materially different.

"The law in Scotland insofar as regards its compulsory enactments, was limited to cases of infirm poor, whether permanently or occasionally so, and did not embrace the case of the able-bodied. That limit amounted to a plain line of distinction as the parties entitled to relief. The limitation operated in a double manner. Poverty alone was not enough, neither was infirmity alone enough. For there must be poverty conjoined with infirmity to entitle a party to relief. Poverty might be the result of mere idleness, drunkenness or dissolute conduct and there was, therefore, no limit or effectual check to it; but infirmity was not under the power or control of parties, to be extended at pleasure; non- age and old age would not come and go at the bidding of parties and even infirmity was not likely to be purposely induced by many in conjunction with poverty.

"This condition of the law had the effect of materially limiting the numbers of the poor were admitted to relief in the one country, as compared to the other and perhaps he had also the effect of stimulating the able-bodied to greater exertion. In the second place, the other characteristic of the Scotch system, that the provision primarily depended on for the poor was the voluntary contributions of the parishioners; that the power of the law had only been called in to aid those contributions where they proved insufficient. Accordingly, there was, in many parts of Scotland, a great reluctance to have recourse to the system of assessment and also reluctance on the part of the poor to receive relief in that shape; and there were not wanting at the present day able and eloquent and pious and benevolent advocates of the system of voluntary contributions as preferable to assessment, both as regards the physical and moral condition of the people. These circumstances might now account for *the different state of matters in the two countries, notwithstanding the apparent similarity of the enactments. The Lord Advocate ventured to say that no proposal could excite more alarm and dissatisfaction among the people of Scotland than a proposal to introduce a Poor Law system similar to that of England. Whatever might be the reason, undoubtedly the feeling prevailed."*

The Lord Advocate said there had been a great influx from the country beyond the efflux from the towns to the country. In many districts, a great change of circumstances had been occasioned by the alteration of the system of management of land. Small farms had been thrown into large farms and the consequence was that there were fewer people able to contribute to the relief of the poor now than formerly. In some extensive localities along the coast, the entire annihilation of the kelp manufacture had thrown many had thrown many persons out of employment and while the means of the contributors had decreased, the funds for relieving the poor had become lessened, the poverty and misery of the labouring classes had materially increased.

The question then was what was to be done to remedy the state of things has proved to exist, resulting as it had done, not from the law as he described it, but from various circumstances? In many parishes the poor did not receive sufficient to support them. As to the actual amount received, there was no test of the relief afforded, unless taken with reference to other circumstances, as the habits of life in the district and the kind of subsistence the applicant would be enabled to obtain by his labour; and the aid of various kinds which he might derive from other sources. The amount of money allowance made by the administrators of poor funds gives, in most cases, but a very imperfect notion of a pauper's resources and the actual means of livelihood. There are very few of those receiving relief in the country parishes who are not able in some way or other to earn a little towards their own subsistence.

It was well known that in Scotland people did not usually possess the same wealth as in England, and it was equally true that the labourers did not live on the same fare. They will more frugal but not less hardy. Nothing could be more erroneous that to test one

A Law is Passed

country by the standard of the other, as gentlemen from this end of the island were apt to do, when they went down at a certain season of the year to occupy the mansions and sport over the manors of Scotch proprietors, forgetting that it was generally the poverty of the one and the wealth of the other that enabled them to do to so enjoy themselves. But after making every allowance for the difference between the two countries, it could not be denied the evils existed which ought to be remedied and the practical question was what a remedy ought to be applied?

It was essential that the means of obtaining relief should be easy; at present no parish was bound to relieve a pauper, except that in which he had a legal settlement; the result of that might be that a serious obstacle was opposed to him. The parish of his settlement might be at a great distance when he wanted the relief, and he might find it difficult or perhaps impossible to reach it. Even when he got there, his claim might be disputed and the result would be litigation, perhaps expensive, to prove his right. Suppose that the parish authorities after meeting to consider his case should refuse to admit his claim, the pauper now had no redress except by going to the Supreme Court-a remedy distant and tedious. And even if these difficulties did not arise, there was still a want of persons whose duty it should be to examine into and look after the condition of the poor in their respective district.

The Lord Advocate proposed he would remove from the pauper the onus of establishing his claim against any other parish. If that parish should seek to relieve itself from the burden, it must do so by ascertaining the parish of settlement against which the claim lies and enforcing that claim. The pauper was not to be the party on whom this duty should devolve. He should get relief from the parish in which he was found, until that parish should have established the liability of a different parish. Having so established that liability, then he proposed that the parish in which the pauper was found should have relief from the parish in which he was found, until that parish found to be liable. This would get rid of all litigation as to the parish ostensibly liable. The arrangement he had to propose would be attended with other advantages; and the issue proposed a pauper should get relief immediately.

Supposing the parish due to give relieve refused to do so, at present more the remedy lay in the Supreme Court. But this means of redress was distant, tedious, expensive and liable to other objections. He proposed that in the first instance the local Sheriff should decide upon the question and if the Sheriff decided in that favour of the applicant, and parish determined to appeal to a higher tribunal, in the meantime the decision so pronounced by the Sheriff should be acted on and the pauper should receive relief. The amount of the relief would be fixed at least by the parochial authorities having their secured the pauper's easy and speedy admission to the roll of persons entitled to relief, the next object was to secure due attention to his case to provide that he should obtain adequate relief. There was at present a want of local activity and constant attention to this point; and there was evident need of some central power to keep local authorities in motion. He proposed in every parish that a person should be appointed, whose duty it would be to attend to the condition of poor, to keep a list of the persons entitled to relief, and to distribute the amount awarded.

He proposed the appointment of the central authority to which local authorities in each parish should make regular reports and which should exercise a general supervision. He had agreed with the commissioners' suggestion that there should be a Board of Supervision in Edinburgh. The Board must be carefully constructed. It should consist of some persons of legal knowledge and men well acquainted in general with the state of society in Scotland and the wants and claims of the poor. The Board, to be efficient, should be composed of men who would bring into it a combination of all these requisites. He proposed three members should be appointed by the Crown. Besides the three, there should be six *ex-officio* members of the Board, the Lord Provost of Edinburgh, the Lord Provost of Glasgow and the Solicitor General of Scotland and for the final three members, he proposed to take the Sheriffs of three of the most important Scotch counties – Perthshire, which he called the Yorkshire of Scotland- of great extent and varied character, partly Highlands and partly Lowland, partly agricultural, partly pasture, partly manufacturing. Another of the Sheriffs he proposed to find in the Sheriff of a large Highland County, in which great destitution was stated at present to prevail – the county of Ross. As a third member, the Sheriff of Renfrewshire – a manufacturing, a mineral and an agricultural county. The Sheriffs of all these counties were resident in Edinburgh. They were all gentlemen of high legal acquirements, and they were also obliged at stated periods to repair to their counties and to mix generally with society there.

He proposed that the Board should have the power of enquiring and investigating generally into all matters connected with the administration of the poor law in all districts. With regard to landward parishes, in addition to the heritors and Kirk Session, there should be associated with them in the management of the poor, a certain number of representatives chosen by the ratepayers. All parishes which were now partly burghal, that is to say a parish in which there was a Royal Burgh, will be treated as a burghal parish and the same principle should also apply to every parish in which there was a Representative to Parliament. He scarcely needed to remind the House that it was the practice of poor persons living in towns to frequently change their residences and a change, though only from street to street, might often be a change from one parish to another. In order to obviate this issue, he would suggest that all the parishes in any town or extended into the parliamentary district of any town and should be formed into a combination of parishes and should be considered as one. so that the settlement obtained in the district as formed, would be a settlement in the place. Another advantage to be derived from this arrangement would be uniting the poorer with the richer portions in each town- thus effecting a more perfect equalisation of the burden of pauperism than existed at present. It would be said, however, that there existed generally a considerable influx from the country into towns, and that as he proposed to afford new facilities for settlement in towns, there might be caused to apprehend an inconvenient accumulation of pauperism in towns. To prevent such a result, it would be proper to extend the period sufficient for the attainment of settlement from three years to seven years. With respect to providing of funds, it had been suggested it should be made compulsory for all parishes to impose an assessment. It was important the manner of assessment should be left as optional as possible. What was suitable or convenient in the circumstances of one parish might not be so in another. It should be an expansive and flexible system.

He now came to the case of lunatics. He did not think that the laws generally relating to lunatics were altogether satisfactory, but this was not the proper occasion for reforming them. With regard to pauper lunatics, he proposed that they should be sent to an asylum of some kind, unless the Board of Supervision should dispense with such removal in any particular case; there were some cases in which such a removal would be cruel, as to deprive a harmless lunatic of the benefits of moving about in good air and of the care of his relations.

The legislation was enacted. In summary, it established:

- Boards of Supervision
- Retention of the parish-based system via Parochial Boards
- Powers for those Boards to raise local taxes.
- Poor relief could be 'outdoor relief' or 'indoor relief' via Poorhouses, which would also aid the sick.
- Parishes should join together to build Poorhouses (Combination Poorhouses)
- An Inspector of the Poor would determine whether applications for relief were legitimate. Unlike England and Wales, the able-bodied poor in Scotland had no automatic right to poor relief.

What was called the 'Workhouse' in England was called the 'Poorhouse' in Scotland. Parochial Boards built poorhouses for those paupers not in receipt of Outdoor Relief. In the second half of the 19th century Boards were given additional powers of registration of births, deaths and marriages and public health. They were abolished in 1894 and replaced with elected Parish Councils. These lasted until 1930, when Edinburgh City Corporation became the poor law authority until the abolition of Poor Laws in 1948, to be replaced by the National Assistance Act.

"Scotch law"

Caricature of Lord Colonsay.
Vanity Fair September 1873.

Sir Henry Littlejohn MD LLD FRSE 1826-1914.

Chapter 2

Something Must Be Done

By the 1860s, it was clear that Edinburgh City's Poorhouse provision was unsuitable, overcrowded and insanitary. The main City Poorhouse, built in 1743, had gradually expanded across the road beside Greyfriars Kirkyard. Attached to it was the Bedlam Madhouse, where the death of the poet Robert Fergusson in squalor had resolved his doctor to set up a hospital to look after the mentally ill with greater respect.

One of the great sons of Edinburgh had an enormous impact on public health in this period; his name was Dr. (later Sir) Henry Littlejohn, now a figure largely forgotten, but whose memory remains in street names on the City Hospital residential development next to the Craiglockhart Poorhouse and whose public health legacy lives on.

In 1862, Littlejohn was appointed Edinburgh's first Medical Officer of Health[8]. At the time many of the city's inhabitants were living in squalid conditions, with minimal sanitation and no water supply. Unsurprisingly, smallpox, typhoid, cholera and diphtheria were common.

In 1865 Littlejohn published a report, analysing conditions in over one thousand separate Edinburgh streets, closes and tenements. It included extensive detail on the most common diseases, as well as historical data on earlier epidemics. The report clearly demonstrated the link between poverty, disease and mortality.

---

8   In order to manage the spread of infectious diseases through the population, Littlejohn campaigned for legal powers to compel medical practitioners to notify all cases of the most infectious diseases. His introduction of compulsory notification of infectious diseases has been described as one of the major advances in public health of the 19th century. He was also one of the first to identify the link between smoking and cancer.

Spurred on by Littlejohn's report, the Lord Provost, William Chambers, and the Town Council launched a widespread programme of urban renewal in Edinburgh. This resulted in the demolition of the worst slums and created the extensive Victorian town that exists today. On Littlejohn's recommendation, the Council also brought in regulations governing water supply, sewage, building standards, food hygiene, waste disposal and the management of cemeteries.

The following account in the *Scotsman* of the Town Council Committee, charged with looking at the condition of the poor, vividly describes not only not the terrible conditions in which many were living, but also the attitudes of the time and how well the 1845 Poor Law was seen to be working.

The Scotsman February 1868
Report on the Lower Classes of Edinburgh

In April last The Lord Provost of Edinburgh called a public meeting of the inhabitants, which was held in the Council Chamber, to consider whether any steps could be taken to simplify, economise and concentrify the action of the public charities in Edinburgh, so as to improve the condition of the really deserving poor. At this meeting, a General Committee was appointed, which subsequently appointed two subcommittees, one of which was to consider the immediate subject contemplated by the Lord Provost, and the other engaged to inquire into the sources and extent of the misery and destitution generally prevailing in certain parts of Edinburgh.

The report of the other committee is a very long and elaborate document, extending to nearly 100 octavo pages, besides an appendix of 20 more. It is full of interesting statistical and other information. In the introduction, the Committee referred to the circumstances which led to the inquiry, remarking on the frequency with which, for many years, attention had been directed to the deplorable condition of our deserving poor. The efforts of Dr. Chalmers and Professor Alison of former years; to the writings and reports of more recent philanthropists; to the appointment of Dr. Littlejohn as Officer of Health and his admirable report on the sanitary condition of the city.

The report itself sets out by describing the import of the phrase "lapsed classes":

It seems to imply that by no violent disruption, by no sudden nor powerful disintegration, but rather by a slow and gradual sliding process, a considerable proportion of the population have lapsed – or fallen away. Fallen away from what? From the class above them; from the purifying influence of the family and home; from the privileges as members of a Christian community; from the social habits and decencies of life; from the source of all real happiness in time, and of all solid hope for eternity? It is well known that such a class exists in considerable numbers in Edinburgh, that its numbers are increasing – partly by additions from the class immediately above it, but chiefly by the fearful rapidity with which a population, freed from the ordinary restraints of prudence and morality, increases, despite the number prematurely swept away both to neglect, want and privation.

The committee state that, in order to make the investigation thoroughly practical, they selected several specimen districts, 15 in number, which are enumerated. They express obligations to Dr. Littlejohn and others for the assistance they received in this selection.

Their investigation, section first, relates to the "lapsed classes, their state and condition"; and sets out with an endeavour to estimate their probable number. From the 20 districts into which Dr. Littlejohn divided Edinburgh, the committee selected the four worst, for the purposes of exhibiting the rate of mortality, the rate of births and the amount of population concentrated in a given area. It appears that the total population of these districts, which are the Canongate, Tron, St Giles and the Grassmarket, amounts to 45,030.

"If we were to deduct from this number all those who circumstances are comfortable and add to it all those from other districts who are in a reverse position, we should probably not materially alter the general result; and therefore, we may ultimately estimate the number at 45,030, or about one fourth of the population. That this is rather than under than over-estimate will be apparent, when it is stated that it is shown by the census of 1861 that 13,209 families, or, allowing the average number to each family, 66,000 individuals, considerably more than one third of our whole population (170,444) per were actually living in houses consisting but of a single room and that 1530 of the single room houses have from six to 15 persons residing in them."

The committee infers that "three classes of society are crowded together in the darkest and most obscure parts of the city, those where they are farthest removed from the observation of the classes above them in the social scale:

a. the abject poor,
b. the abandoned,
c. the criminal,

who form, accordingly, the bulk of the population in the four districts specified. They add that the information received from intelligent criminal officers goes to show that the great majority of those convicted for crime in Edinburgh come from these districts. By the visitors who procured the information from the districts selected was information obtained on the following subjects:

1. the state of the family,
2. the state of the dwelling,
3. the state of education of the children,
4. the state of attendance on church".

In regard to the state of the district, the report remarks upon "the natural sanitary advantages of Edinburgh, the open and elevated character of which gives the town a free ventilation and a command of fresh and pure air for such as few cities possess; while there are other excesses which ought to make it one of the healthiest of towns, but for the singular errors of its construction, which have more than counteracted its natural advantages." The committee also remark that," Edinburgh, in proportion to its population, covers a larger area than almost any town in Britain. This description however is only applicable to the New Town. In the more densely peopled districts of the older parts of the city are to be found an amount of overcrowding, with its natural concomitant of vice and disease, which are not surpassed, if they are equalled, by any town in Britain.

Something Must Be Done

There is no city in the empire where the inhabitants are more closely packed together in some districts, where there is a higher death-rate, more disease, more abject poverty, more vice and wretchedness than are sheltered in the miserable dens of the Old Town, which are seldom visited by the well-to-do inhabitants of our palatial abodes.

"While in such districts as those of the Lower New Town or Broughton, the mortality is only 15.47, or 17, respectively per 1000, or in the district of the Grange it falls even to 13.78 per 1000, in the Grassmarket it is 32.5, in the Tron at 34.55 or in the aggregate 39; or, as Dr. Littlejohn shows, in some particular closes in actually reaches 60 per 1000. Nor is it difficult to account for this. In the Lower New Town, the population is only 95.4 per acre; in the New Town, 21.2; in the Grange, 7.5; In the Grassmarket it is 237.6; in the Canongate 206.7; in the Tron, 340 – a density of population in some of these districts unequalled in any town in Britain".

"And the census for 1861 brought out distinctly that in Edinburgh, despite its boasted piety and refinement, there were actually 13,209 families living in houses of but a single room: these families comprehending 66,000 individuals, or considerably more than one third of our whole population. Of these rooms inhabited by a whole family, the number of inmates varying from 6 to 15 in each, 121 had no windows and, from later police return, upwards of 900 were cellars, most of them had damp and utterly dark!"

"It must not be supposed that the 13,000 families embrace the vicious[9] and abject poor only. Among the numbers are to be found nearly all of our common labouring class, who are compelled by the impossibility of obtaining houses of a better construction or in a more healthy locality, to dwell in 'dens' where cleanliness is impossible, decency is necessarily constantly outraged and the laws of health are hourly violated – nay, cannot by any possibility be observed".

"As a necessary consequence, the epidemics which assail us from time to time find in such localities their fitting hot-beds where they germinate and from whence their prolific seeds are diffused over the whole town."

---

9   'Vicious' in this sense meant immoral i.e. prone to vice

"While a population in such a state of degradation is a disgrace to any civilised community, it is also a prolific source of danger and expense. The unkempt, untaught children who today swarm about our streets will become in are very few years the tramps and vagrants and criminals at our doors. In these unwholesome dwellings are generated the epidemics which ever and anon break forth, carrying death and desolation in their course. Chiefly for such a population are jails, prisons, and police offices provided, and all the machinery of our criminal law are put in operation. They necessitate the erection of hospitals and poorhouses, and tax the resources of our dispensaries to minister to their wants, when stricken down by disease. For them chiefly are our innumerable charities organized; and it has been estimated that on them throughout the United Kingdom is actually spent a sum more than sufficient to pay the interest of the National Debt."

Second section treats of the "*causes which had produced the present deplorable state of matters.*" The first of these is *that the classes referred to are crowded together without association with a better class*; the second that *they are neglected by our law-givers and also by their employers*; the third is *their outgrowal of Christianising influences*; and the fourth is their *want of education.*

Under this head, the Committee says:

"All evidence goes to show that the pauper and criminal classes are the worst educated class in the community. The following table shows that of 239 boys and girls under 16 years of age who were convicted of, or committed for crimes during 1866, only one could read and write well, 98 could not write and 54 could neither read nor write. Of 951 criminals above 16 years of age, only 53 could read and write well, 356 could not write and 183 he could neither read nor write."

Fifth cause *Intemperance*. The evil effects of this vice are enumerated as follows:

a. It produces neglected education among the children, by taking the money for drink that should pay for schooling.

b. It destroys the comfort of the home. Bit by bit the furniture that adorns the little apartment disappears to satisfy the insatiable craving; and when drink becomes a necessity, home comforts cannot be procured.
c. It brutalises the person addicted to it.
d. It is a great cause of crime.
e. It pauperises. Mr. William Clark, Inspector of the Poor at Aberdeen says "In more than half the cases in which parochial relief is applied for, the necessity for it arises from dissipated habits, either of the parties themselves or of the parents who ought to support them. The money which we pay to away in relief is often taken at once to the whisky shop. It often happens that the mother of a number of children extends the allowance in whisky, commits a breach of the peace and is sent to prison. The children are thrown on our hands and we are frequently obliged to pay a second time for their support in the Industrial School. The offence of deserting wives and children is much on increase. In most cases I could show that the offender is wasting upon drink more than sufficient to support his family."

The sixth cause is *drinking customs and other causes leading to intemperance.*

The seventh is *the licensing system,* the whole of which, the committee say," requires consideration and some general principles should be laid down for the guidance of those with whom the responsibility of granting licences lies."

The eighth cause is *pawnbroking.* "Husbands pawn their wives' clothes, and wives those of their husbands and children-bedding, household furniture, everything that gives character and comfort to house soon disappears. Again, trusting then any special pressure will be met by raising a loss on their household effects, improvidence is encouraged and workmen in receipt of good wages are tempted to spend them all in dissipation; and when sickness or accident, short time, or dissertation make an extra call for money, the children's clothes go first to the pawnbroker's, rendering it impossible for them to attend school."

The ninth cause, which is gone into at great length, is *the operation of the Poor Law*. The evil effects of its operation are enumerated and illustrated at great length under the following heads.

It takes the earnings of the industrious to support the idle and or dissolute.

It makes no distinction between that poverty to which is resulted from misfortune and that which has originated in vice.

It tends to diminish industry by giving to a pauper a right to maintenance whenever he sinks to a certain depth.

It tends to diminish frugality, and relax the improvident habits of our labouring classes, by leading them to trust for support for the future rather to legal provision than to the efforts of their own prudence and carefulness.

It destroys the ties of relationship. It leads parents to desert their children and children in their turn to neglect their parents. "It has thus," says Dr Chalmers, "poisoned the strongest affections of nature, and turned inwardly towards the indulgence of what an absorbent selfishness those streams, which else would have flowed out on the needy of our own blood and our own kindred."

It has lessened the sympathy of the wealthier for the poorer classes by giving the latter a legal claim on the former.

It has destroyed the sympathy and aid which even the poor naturally extend to one another.

It has tended to destroy, in a great measure, one of the great peculiarities of our Scottish education. In 1816, one who had carefully studied the subject, writes, "*While in the southern division of the kingdom, poorhouses and other charitable establishments for the reception of the aged and indigent come down like extinguishers on the better feelings of the heart, debarring the grandchild, and the niece, and the nephew from sharing the company, taking advantage of the experience, or clinging in childish fondness round the knees of age....*"

It tends to cause the working classes to leave or be driven from the rural districts, and to settle in the town, rendering it more difficult to get suitable labour in the former, and tending greatly to increase the unproductive population in the latter.

Tends to increase enormously the number of the poor and the expense of maintaining them.

It appears that before the imposition of the Poor Law in Scotland, the whole sum required for the support of the poor was £155,121 12 shillings and two pence; and that these funds were administered by 7542 persons giving their services gratuitously, and by 532 paid agents, of whom 330 were employed in levying the funds and 202 in the management of the poor.

No sooner did the Poor Law come into operation, than an immediate rise took place. In 1846, £295,232 were expended, while during the year ending 14 May 1866, the expenditure was £783,127. In 1867 in reached the sum of £807,631 five shillings and sixpence halfpenny.

The tenth cause is *indiscriminate private charity*. "Your committee are satisfied, from all the enquiries they have made, that there is no surer way to minister to the worst vices of the lapsed classes than indiscriminate almsgiving, either by individuals or societies. Those who openly solicit alms are notoriously the idle and the vicious, and every penny carelessly bestowed in this way of promiscuous charity is only fostering their idleness and vice".

The eleventh cause is the *want of method among the charitable societies*. "The great array of societies apparently founded to meet every want and to relieve every form of distress, would lead any observer of the surface of things to suppose that in no country is benevolence carried farther, and in no town could there be less suffering than in ours. And yet those who have practical knowledge of the work among the poor will be the first to admit that, for want of that thorough system and method which we apply to our business affairs, the administration of charity is in a most unsatisfactory and confused state. The agencies of the existing societies are, with few exceptions, totally inadequate to maintain the frequent and systematic visitation of the poor in their own homes, by which alone that knowledge of their character and habits can be obtained, which is indispensable, on the one hand, to guard against imposition and, on the other, to discover the really deserving, and to ascertain their actual requirements. Nor is this all the evil, for owing to the want of communication between the various societies regarding those whom they assist. Many persons obtain aid from several institutions, while others were less clamorous, but often more deserving, are left in want".

The twelfth cause is *overcrowding*.

The thirteenth, *want of water.*

The fourteenth, *want of light.*

The fifteenth, *want of proper arrangements for removing offensive matter.*

In concluding this section, the committee again remark on the "evils engendered by the overlapping of public and private charities".

"From the absence of all harmonious action and systematic communication between the agents of these charities, the same individuals, if brazen-faced and impudent, or if cunning and hypocritical, often obtain aid from several individuals or public charities, while others, who are more modest and retiring, and generally more deserving, are left without assistance. It would be a difficult task to estimate the waste of resources on the one hand and the encouragement of idleness, fraud, intemperance and every vice on the other, which results from the utter ignorance of the directors of one public charity regarding the relief which is afforded by those of another."

It was clear something had to be done. This was a period of great Victorian confidence in public works and building, but much of medieval Edinburgh in the Old Town was squalid, insanitary and downright dangerous. For example, over Paisley Close on the Royal Mile, there is a sculptured head of a boy with the inscription 'Heave awa chaps, I'm no dead yet!' commemorating the collapse of a tenement in 1861. Inhabited by 77 people, 35 died. The monument commemorates the discovery of a twelve-year-old boy still alive in the rubble. This incident is regarded as having been the catalyst for action and 1867 The Edinburgh City Improvement Act, conceived in the wake of Littlejohn's report, initiated the rebuilding of the Old Town and the clearing away of swathes of substandard (albeit historic) buildings.

This was a period of grand designs. In 1870, the first Princes Street railway station opened (replaced in 1893 by Waverley Station), the great Gothic chateau of Fettes College opened, Chambers Street was laid, and work began on the new Royal Infirmary, the biggest hospital in Europe under one roof. The City's poorhouses were to be replaced and consolidated by two large model poorhouses, Craigleith Hospital and Poorhouse in the west of the City (opened in 1868, later developing into today's Western General Hospital) and to the South West, the Craiglockhart Poorhouse.

Chapter 3

The New Poorhouse

It was clear not everyone could agree on the location of the new Poorhouse.

From a letter to the Scotsman[10]

Sir- a copy of Saturday's *Courant* was sent gratuitously to each of the ratepayers in the Fifth Ward. Some of them were rather puzzled to account for such a gift; but an inspection of the paper showed that it contained a report of the speech extending to four and a half-printed columns delivered by Mr. Curror at a meeting of the Fifth Ward. It may be inferred that it was from Mr. Curror's desire not to hide his light under a bushel, that they are indebted for so valuable a gift. In the long and laboured special pleading referred to, an attempt is made to show the necessity for the erection of a new city poorhouse in the country, some 10 miles from Edinburgh and in connection therewith, it is proposed to purchase 500 acres of "unimproved muirland", which the inmates of the poorhouse are to cultivate. The cost of the whole is estimated at £30,000 which, according to Mr. Curror, is to be liquidated by 1d. per pound being added to the poor rates for 30 years; while according to the report by the House Committee, 1½ d. per pound is required for the above purpose-a difference betwixt the two estimates of which no explanation is given, which goes to show the loose and unsatisfactory data are on which the proposal proceeds.

The employment of pauper labour profitably is a principle on which the purchase of land is based. It is said on higher authority that when a man wishes to build a house, he sets about counting the cost thereof, but no such qualms trouble Mr. Curror. He lays it down as an axiom that "all men are born gardeners" – ergo the inmates of our poorhouse, " *the aged and other friendless impotent poor*", to use the words of the

---

10   The Scotsman October 1861.

Act, and *"those poor persons, who from weakness, facility of mind or by reason of dissipated or improvident habits are unable to take charge of their own affairs"* are forthwith, in virtue of their inherent capabilities as "born gardeners", to be quite fit for the work of ploughing, digging, trenching and draining some 500 or 100 acres, as the case may be, of unimproved muirland. No greater cruelty can be conceived than enforcing aged and broken-down paupers to execute work for which they are entirely unfitted; and before bringing under the notice of the public such a speculation, the first step should have been to have instituted an enquiry into the capabilities of the inmates for the work in which it was proposed to employ them; but nothing of this kind has been done. Everyone knows that farm labour, even to those bred to it, is very severe and the experience of all our colonies show that the inhabitants of towns are quite unfitted for the task-breaking stones on the highway being the nearest approximation in that direction to which any of them have attained.

The statistics which Mr. Curror has given of some cases where land is cultivated in connection with poorhouses do not apply. In these the land merely consisted of a few acres, if the soil is good, it could be cultivated for the rearing of vegetables without much difficulty; but in the present case a large farm is evidently contemplated.

There is one other point worthy of attention, the importance of which Mr. Curror clearly sees. The difficulty which attends getting suitable parties to represent the Wards of the Poor Law Board is well known. Few men in business can spend the necessary time. This difficulty would be enormously increased were the poorhouse to be removed 10 miles from Edinburgh. Mr. Curror says it occupies in 20 minutes to walk from his home to the present poorhouse and that the distance of 10 miles by railway it would be accomplished in a quarter of an hour *"therefore less time would be consumed by taking the house 10 miles out of town by railway than by keeping it where it is"*. He entirely forgets however that in the first place you must walk or hire a cab to the railway: -for a distance very little short of the poorhouse, even from his house. Then, instead of travelling 10 miles in a quarter of an hour, it would take nearly double that time by any ordinary train. Finally, it would depend upon the proximity of the model farm to the railway, whether a mile or two might not require to be travelled after arriving

The New Poorhouse

at the nearest station. Again, on return, as trains do not wait on even Poor Law Guardians, an hour or two might elapse before the arrival of the return train. In short, the best part of the day would be consumed in attending a meeting at the Edinburgh country poorhouse, to say nothing of the want of supervision by the Guardians distance should create and the expense attending such trips.

It is stated that no addition of officials is contemplated, but if the present poorhouse is to be retained for certain purposes to the extent of one half, it is difficult to understand how both departments are to be managed by the present staff officials.

I trust the Fifth Ward will, at their meeting tonight, put an extinguisher on Mr. Curror's pet scheme, the paternity of which is well known.

I am etc.
H

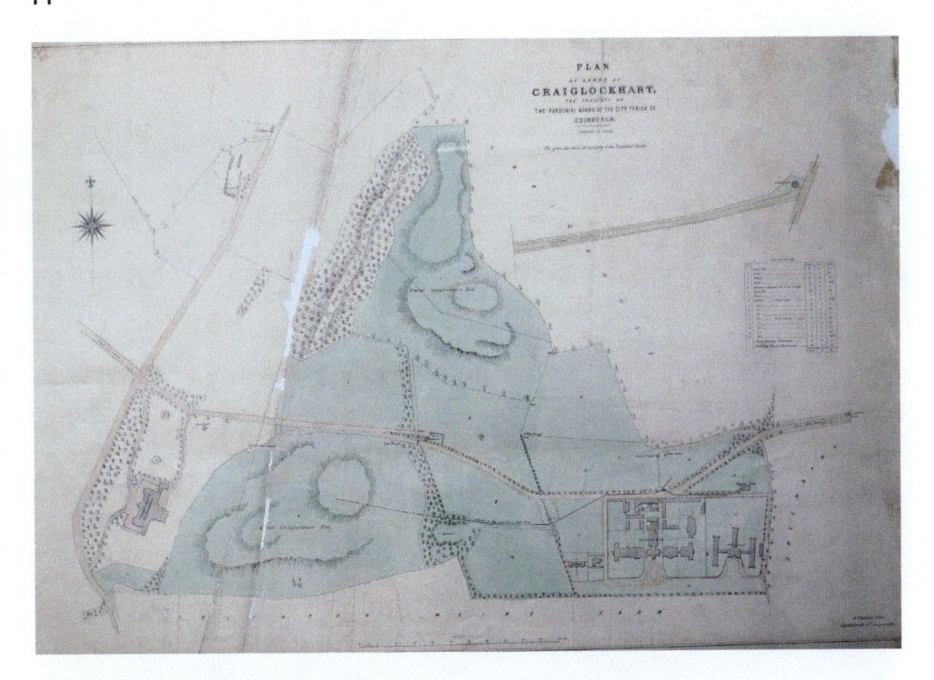

Map showing the property boundary of the lands acquired by the Parochial Board from the Craiglockhart Estate.

The Poorhouse administrative building today.

The New Poorhouse

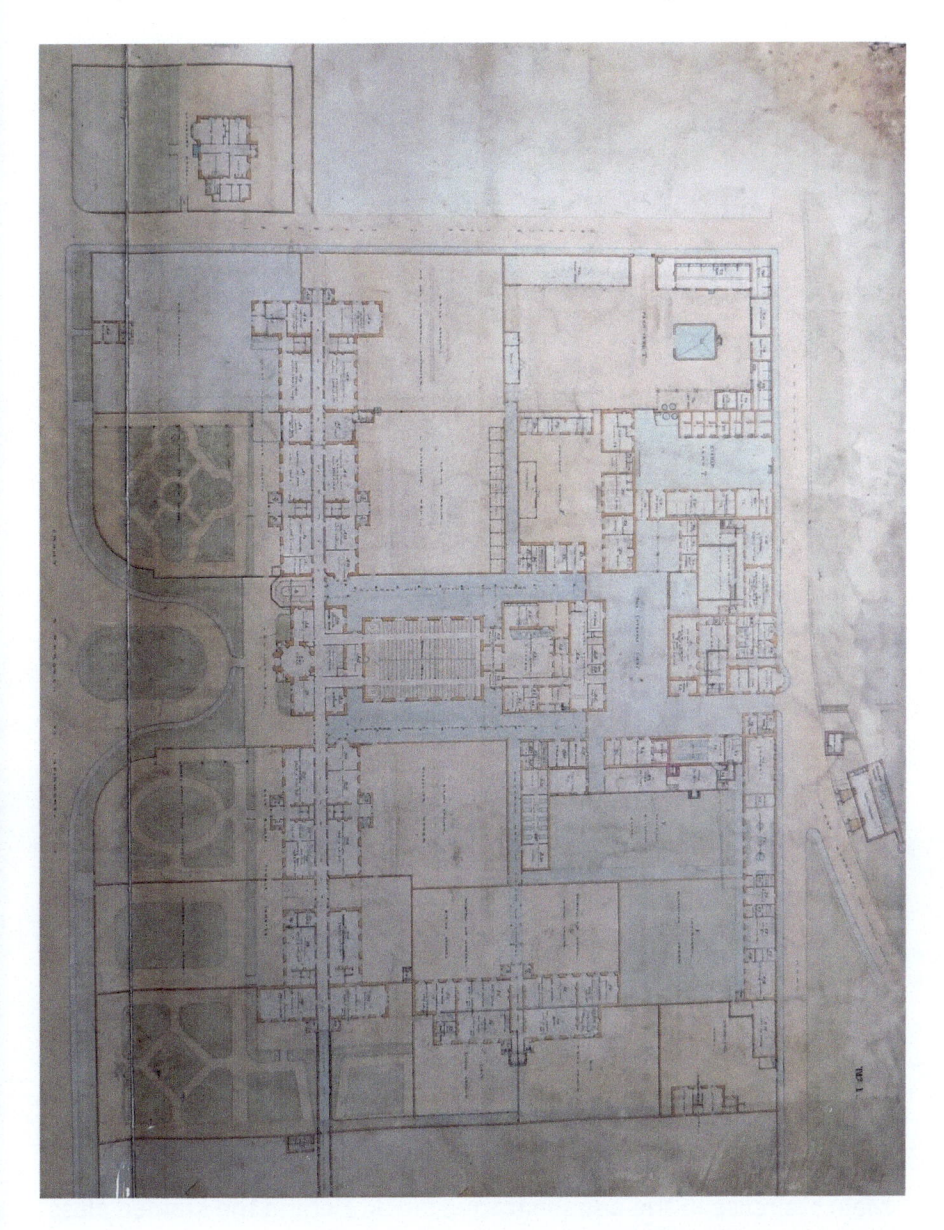

The Poorhouse site plans.
Note the corridor running through the whole complex.
By kind permission Edinburgh City Archives.

Main staircase in the administrative block. Behind the stained glass was the dining hall, which, at this end, also functioned as a chapel.

The prospect of the new Poorhouse is referred to in The Orkney Herald in January 1866, recording a farm servant's speech. Witty and entertaining, it gives a lively insight into the family economics of the period.

A farm servant's speech

A meeting of farm servants was held at Davidson's Mains near Edinburgh on Thursday week for the purpose of forming the Mid Lothian Farm Servants Protection Society. The object of the association is to obtain a rise of wages for farm servants.

In the course of the proceedings, Thomas Ewing, farm servant, Myreside, rose amidst cheers and said- *"Weel, you mann forg'ie me;* the chairman's ta'en the bite oot o'my teeth (Laughter). Having heard from a sonsy ploughman aboot someone writing aboot the progressional condition o'ploughmen. (Cheers), I here give a brief statement for myself; I am being a ploughman near the enlightened city. (Cheers) My fee is £22 a year, with twa pecks o'meal per week, whiles very inferior indeed (laughter and cheers) – wi' a forpet o'tatties for each day. (Cheers) Noo' takin' rations and wages thegither – no speakin' o the hoose, for it's a heavy rent to risk your living in't- I think it amounts to £29 4s and if we reduce that sum to weekly, I think it comes to 1s 10½d for six o' a family. That's puir pauper's allowance (Laughter and cheers) I think the sooner Craiglockhart Poorhouse is built the better (Laughter and cheers) We'll mak' gran' hands at hoeing the strawberries. (Renewed laughter and cheers). Now, tak' oot o' oor small deposit o' fee five shillings per week for groceries- a heavy pack indeed for the wife to carry frae Edinburgh for six o' a family- (laughter and cheers) no including soor dook [11] hauf mixed wi' water (Laughter).

As the Soor Dook Poet describes it-

"They've sell't soor dook here all my time
To fill their nasty greedy purse
Clear water thus, half whitened syne
And has to take it with their curse" (laughter and cheers).

---

11 Soor dook was buttermilk. A daily sight in Edinburgh were milkmaids on horseback riding into town with soor dook barrels strapped across the saddle behind them. There were also soor dook carts and stances around the Old Town.

Now also tak' oot o' our fee 38s 11d for coal, 10s for light, forby doctor's expenses and education.

Yes, I have known men who have been faithful servants from twenty to nearly thirty years in one place, and when they became stiff though bondage of toil, torn with rheumatics though winter's blast, infirm though hard labour, the unconscionable master passed the tyrannical verdict upon them "Depart from me, you will soon turn a pauper upon my hand". (Cheers) There is no pension to cheer their old age – no consolation given to their bereaved souls to be left to rot and decay amid the wearied injustice of care (cheers)

Another article refers to the same speech...

In his pathetic picture of a ploughman's wages, which are all he has to maintain a family of six, he remarked that was a poor pauper's allowance. The sooner Craiglockhart Poorhouse was built the better. They would make grand hands at hoeing the strawberries! This tickled the meeting vastly and was therefore received with laughter. No wonder. Thomas himself evidently enjoyed his own joke. Fancy a Scotch ploughman longing for the paradise of the Poorhouse! The idea seemed perfectly delectable to the audience and they could not choose but giggle at its sublime absurdity. Catch our Scotch peasantry going into the Poorhouse so long as the world is open to them for immigration. Nature cannot afford to waste such precious materials on poorhouses when she has new empires to build up and we have a notion that if the ploughmen do not succeed in their efforts at improvement, many of them will probably drop off to other fields and pastures across where they have been long expected. This will leave more room on better wages for those who remain.

In due course the Poorhouse was built. The following two articles provide a vivid description of the enterprise, reflecting the industry and ingenuity of the time.

The Craiglockhart Poorhouse foundation stone was to be laid with great ceremony in 1867.

The Daily Review July 1867
The New City Poorhouse

The foundation stone of the new Edinburgh City Poorhouse is to be laid on Thursday with full Masonic honours. A large gathering of the brethren of the mystic tie is expected from all parts of Scotland and we understand that a considerable number of American citizens who are visiting this country and who belong to the Brotherhood are also to take part in the procession and ceremonial. Our readers, especially those in town, will expect from us some more detailed description of the building which is to be in publicly inaugurated and it will add to the interest in the ceremony of Thursday if we give the description now.

The new Edinburgh City Poorhouse is being erected upon the south-eastern portion of the estate of Craiglockhart, distant about two and a half miles from Edinburgh. The situation is a very pleasant and healthy one and has all the fresh air, quietness and seclusion of a country site within a short distance of the city. The poorhouse is placed upon one of the lower parts of West Craiglockhart Hill and faces the South. The ground falls both to the front and back which will keep the new buildings dry which renders drainage easy and successful. From the front windows a fine view is obtained of the Pentland hills and the richly wooded country about Dreghorn and Bonaly. The view to the North and East is one of the most beautiful and most extensive in the neighbourhood of Edinburgh. In the foreground lie spread out Morningside and the numerous residential villas about the Grange; while beyond between Blackford Hill and Arthur's Seat, a magnificent vista is obtained of the Firth of Forth embracing even the Bass Rock at the German Ocean.

The new Poorhouse is situated about half a mile to the south of the Morningside Asylum and access can be got to it either by the road from Morningside to Penicuik or by that from Edinburgh to Colinton. The principal carriage approach will be from Morningside starting from the Penicuik Road about half a mile beyond the Morningside toll bar. A handsome lodge and gateway will be placed at this entrance. A new access to the Poorhouse has been formed from the Colinton

Road. The new road starts at Craiglockhart farmhouse, passes by the side of an old keep now partly in ruins, and, proceeding up the valley between East and West Craiglockhart Hills, rises by an easy ascent to the new buildings. This road will also have a Porter Lodge and gateway and will be that most used by the paupers and for the general working of the establishment. Various other roads are being formed within and across the grounds, and when the whole is completed, upwards of two miles of new roads will have been constructed.

The Poorhouse will have 36 acres of ground in connection with it. Of this about 16 acres will be occupied by buildings and enclosed courts. The remaining 20 acres will be brought under cultivation by the paupers, agricultural labour at Craiglockhart being made to supersede to a certain extent the less healthy indoor employments usual in poorhouses. It is contemplated afterwards to take in East Craiglockhart Hill which joins on to the Poorhouse grounds. This will be tastefully laid out with terraces and walks and, as a cemetery will be required in connection with the Poorhouse, it is possible that if this locality is found suitable, it may be placed here.

As there is an abundance of superior building stone upon the Board's estate, two quarries have been opened up for the erection of the new buildings. One of these, at the side of Colinton Road produces a stone of a red colour, very similar to that of which the old Castle or keep is built. The other quarry is upon the site of the buildings and for working it the contractor has laid down a railway which, as the quarry is situated on higher ground, and the loaded trucks will descend by their own weight, will considerably facilitate the carriage of the stone. This stone which will be employed in the external faces of the walls is of a uniform bluish tint and exceedingly hard compact and close in the grain. It promises to be a very durable stone and will remain uninjured by exposure to the weather for a lengthened period. The hewn work is of the yellow rock from Redhall Quarry and its warmer hue will form a pleasing contrast with the cool blueish shade of the rubble work executed with the Craiglockhart stone. Sand and clay have also been discovered on the site and are being opened up for use in the new buildings.

The new Poorhouse faces the south and the principal front looking in this direction extends over above 1200 feet. It is broken up into three distinct buildings – the main Poorhouse in the centre, the Infirmary to the East and the lunatic asylum to the West. The new buildings are in the Scotch style, treated in a simple and inexpensive way and the bold corbelling and crowstepped gables will harmonise well with the somewhat rugged and mountainous scenery which surrounds them. The principal effect will be obtained from the arrangement of the plan, with bold projections and deep recesses giving great variety of light and shade and a picturesque skyline. A lofty corbelled tower, octagonal in form, and 105 feet high, marks the centre of the main Poorhouse and projecting wings at either end give firmness and character to the extreme.

Main Poorhouse

The main Poorhouse is designed upon the block system, the building being subdivided into a number of separate blocks, connected with the centre and each other by a service corridor. The block system is so superior to any other in the sanitary point of view and also as a safeguard from fire, that its adoption in the case of buildings with a large number of inmates is becoming very general. There is another special reason for adoption in the case of a large poorhouses. In poorhouses the separation of the various classes is a matter of vital moment and there is no way in which this could be so simply and so effectively by secured as by the block system. Each class is placed on its own block, with its own airing ground attached and is thus entirely isolated from the others.

The main Poorhouse consists of five blocks to the front – the two West blocks for the male paupers and the centre one for the administration and the officials and the two East blocks for the female paupers. The females, being more numerous than the males, have another block to the rear of those in front and facing eastwards. The buildings are three storeys in height, the ground floor being occupied as day rooms and the two upper floors as dormitories.

A spacious service corridor runs down the centre from end to end at the level of each floor. This corridor is lighted and ventilated by large windows between every block and is broken up into short stretches, and the usual dinginess and closeness of along corridor is entirely avoided. The central corridor will be used for the general working of establishment, only passed through it under charge of the officials to or from the dining-hall.

The day rooms and dormitories are placed on either side of the central corridor and are spacious apartments 35 feet long by 19 feet wide and 12 high. In the dormitories the cubic airspace per head is on the average about 500 feet. As the various classes of paupers required to be isolated, each ward is made complete within itself. Each has its own day room, its own dormitories, a separate staircase and special airing-ground. The male paupers are divided into four classes- old men of good character, doubtful old men, dissolute men and boys: and the females into seven classes – old women of good character, married women, doubtful old women, girls, children under five and infants. It was at first intended to have another class; viz. married couples who were to be accommodated in cottages with a small garden attached to each. The Board of Supervision, however, did not consider that this was consistent with the present Poor Law Act and the idea has been abandoned for the present.

The sanitary appliances for each Ward are placed in external projections, which, besides being thoroughly lighted and ventilated themselves, are cut off by lobbies from the wards. Each Ward is provided at every floor with baths, lavatories and water closets, all of the best and most durable description. In addition to this, there is provided in the internal court ease of access, a large general bathing establishment, where a considerable number can be bathed at the same time. The general bathroom is a lofty apartment, lighted from the roof and having in connexion dressing and undressing rooms, so that bathing may go on with regularity and dispatch. Immediately behind the administrative block is placed the common Dining Hall. This is seated for 600 paupers and in the meantime may also be used as a church. As this is not desirable, however, it is probable that a separate church will be erected on the ground to the south of the main Poorhouse.

Behind the Dining Hall, but separated by a serving room and lobby, is placed the kitchen department. In addition to the ordinary cooking ranges, the kitchen will be fitted up with a number of steam cooking vessels in which a large portion of the food will be prepared. Vegetables for example will be placed in open wire trays and cooked by steam, both better and quicker than could be done by the ordinary process of boiling in water. Behind the kitchen department is the storekeeper's office with the various storerooms in close proximity.

At the back of the internal female airing courts is placed the washing department and an enclosed drying and bleaching green. The washing-house will be fitted up with the most perfect steam washing and drying apparatus, supplied from the steam boilers which are in the immediate vicinity, and which also supply the steam cooking vessels, pump the water up to the great tower and heat the hot water required for the baths etcetera. A bakehouse with two capacious ovens will prepare the bread used in the poorhouse. At the back of the internal male courts are the workshops for smiths, carpenters, plumbers, painters, tailors, shoemakers, bookbinders etcetera and adjoining them extensive farm offices with byre, stabling, cart sheds etc. A porter's lodge and probationary wards are placed beside the back entrance gate. Here the newly arrived paupers will be received and examined, before being admitted into the house. Proper waiting and examination rooms, baths, lavatories clothes stores, and disinfecting apparatus are provided.

Infirmary

The Infirmary is designed upon the pavilion system, now universally adopted in all new hospitals. There are four pavilions arranged in pairs for ordinary cases and a fifth pavilion at the back to be used exclusively as a fever hospital. At the centre of the corridor, which connects the pavilions, is placed the administrative block, which contains the officials' apartments, the dispensary storerooms and kitchen departments.

The pavilions are two storeys in height and contain one ward on each floor. The ordinary wards are 60 feet by 22 feet and the fever wards 86 feet by 23 feet. They are lighted by large windows on both sides and careful provision is made for their thorough ventilation at all times. The lavatories baths and water closets are placed upon the external angles at one end of the pavilions. This position secures thorough ventilation, indispensable in such a case and they are further cut off from the wards by intervening lobbies. The ward scullery and the nurse's room are at the other end of the ward and the nurse can at all times command the patients by a window from her own room. The Infirmary has its own washing house, laundry and bleaching green. The special airing grounds for the Infirmary extend to four acres and will be laid out in grass and shrubbery with proper walks, so that convalescent patients may at any time enjoy half an hour's sunshine.

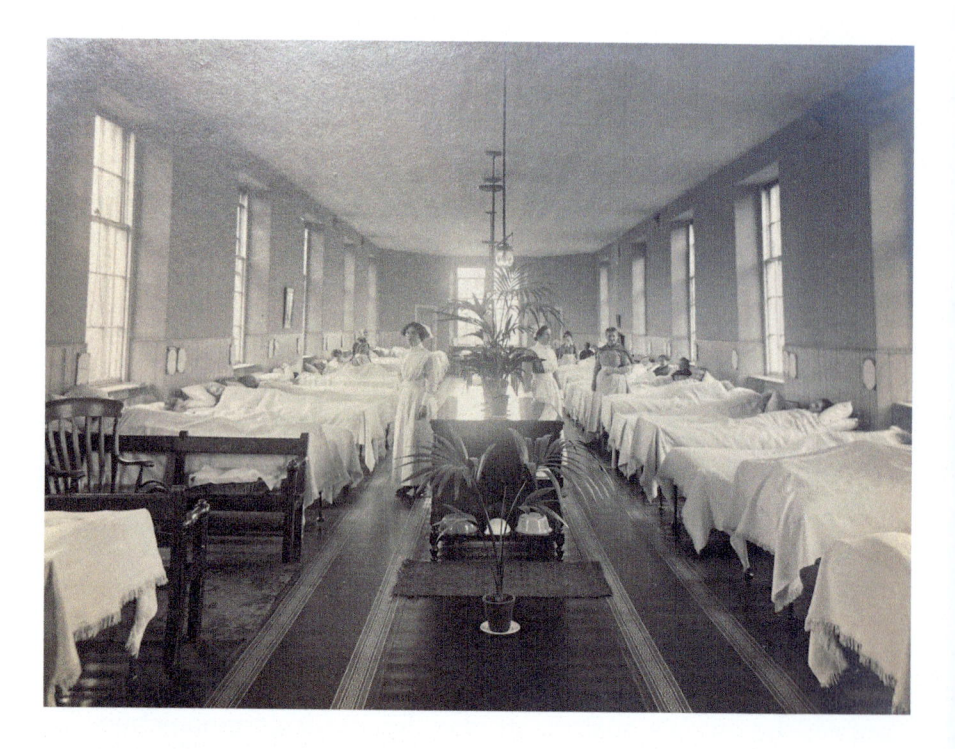

Lunatic asylum

The Lunatic Asylum is to the west of the poor house up on the higher ground and faces the South. It is a building 300 feet long with a projecting centre and wings at either end. The centre will be occupied

The New Poorhouse

by the officials, having the male lunatics to the East and the females to the West. The building is two stories in height, the ground floor being occupied as day rooms and the upper floor as dormitories. A few single bedrooms are provided on the ground floor for quiet and feeble patients and also a general bathing establishment for each sex. A handsome dining and recreation hall is placed at the centre of the building behind the officials' apartments. The dormitory floor is partly laid out in large and airy associated dormitories and partly in single rooms. The water closets and lavatories are placed in projections and separated from the wards by well ventilated lobbies. Proper workshops are provided for the males, and a washing house and laundry with proper steam apparatus for the females.

The Lunatic Asylum, with the airing grounds in connection with it, will cover upwards of five acres, but in the meantime, it has been delayed and is not included in the present contract.

A Chapel for divine service is not included in the present contract and if none be erected, the Dining Hall will be made use of for this purpose. It is likely however that a church will be built upon the ground to the South of the poorhouse at the side of the principal approach. It has generally been found to have a beneficial effect upon the inmates, and to improve their behaviour during the service to have a church, a distinct building external to the poor house.

The Governor of the Poorhouse will be accommodated in a detached villa in the grounds. As the Edinburgh Water Companies Act did not permit them to sell water to the poorhouse, it became necessary to obtain a supply from another source. This will be got from a spring on the Craiglockhart estate, close to the Poorhouse grounds. A reservoir will be constructed to store 300,000 gallons, so that there may be no chance of the supply running short in dry weather. A steam engine will pump the water to a large iron cistern in the upper part of the central tower and from thence it will be distributed by gravitation to the whole buildings. The poorhouse will manufacture its own gas and for this purpose a small gas work will be erected on the north side of the grounds.

Adjacent to the gas work, the whole sewerage of the poorhouse will be collected in covered filtering tanks and made available for agricultural purposes. The manure not required for the poorhouse grounds will be readily disposed of to neighbouring farmers. The total number of pauper females for whom accommodation is provided is 1150 – 750 in the main poorhouse, 250 in the Infirmary and 100 in the lunatic asylum. The total cost of the Poorhouse, Infirmary and the Governor's house at present contracted for is £35,000 pounds Sterling in addition to which about £2000 pounds is required for roads. The whole buildings will be completed for occupancy by the 1st of April 1869.

The great foundation stone laying ceremony was duly recorded with dramatic illustration in the press. However, journalistic rivalries clearly existed, as can be seen in this early charge of "fake news".

The Grand Masonic Procession.

The North Briton Saturday, July 27th, 1867
The Late Masonic Procession

As an example of how some of the cheap illustrated periodicals get up their cuts to order, we may refer to the picture which appears in the Illustrated Weekly News of Saturday last, of the Grand Masonic Procession in Edinburgh. The ordinary columns of the paper contain a brief account of the ceremony of laying the foundation stone of Edinburgh's Poorhouse at Craiglockhart on the 4th Inst. with the notice that the illustration represents the procession on its way to Craiglockhart. The illustration in question, which occupies a whole page, an immense body, represents the Masonic Brethren in the course of being marshalled in front of Holyrood Palace. The ground is kept by the Hussars, and in the rear, we see the "bearskins" of the household troops. The fountain of the outer quadrant quadrangle has evidently obtained leave of absence and on the northwest side of the palace the railing has disappeared and the prodigious crowds which have overborne the artist's imagination are packed close up to the sculptured doorway of the nave of the chapel. The balconies and battlements of the palace are crowded to excess with excited spectators waving hats and handkerchiefs at the sight. The whole picture is highly sensational, and the artist has been lavish in his effects. Now the curiosity of the business is that the Masonic procession of the 4th Inst. was not at any moment within a mile and a half of Holyrood, the muster ground (except for the Grand Lodge, which met at the Freemasons' Hall) having been Bruntsfield Links.

The Scotsman August 1869
Letters to the editor
The New City Poorhouse

The new City Poorhouse at Craiglockhart which we had yesterday an opportunity of inspecting, is now very nearly completed and, in the course of a few weeks, probably six, will be in for occupation. The time has therefore now arrived when a description of the building may be fairly attempted, for although the plans were fully explained in these columns at the time the work was commenced, now more than two years ago, it is much more satisfactory to deal with the actual structure and to state what really has been done in preference to what is merely preparatory. A good deal of work yet requires to be executed out of doors in the way of making roads and forming yards and approaches, but very little remains to be done in the building itself and indeed some portions of it are already being furnished.

We may briefly call to mind the circumstance that the erection of a new poorhouse by the City Parochial Board was rendered necessary in consequence of the old charity workhouse at Forrest Road having been condemned by the Board of Supervision. The Craiglockhart Estate coming into the market and offering excellent facilities for the purposes of the poorhouse, it was secured by the Board, who have every reason to congratulate themselves on the purchase. The site is within a very short distance of the city and yet the scene is as quiet and is thoroughly secluded as if it were miles away. The new buildings are erected on the south eastern portion of the estate up on the spur of West Craiglockhart Hill, along which they extend for about 400 yards. The ground slopes away both to the front and back and affords excellent facilities for thorough drainage. A more picturesque site could not have been chosen for the most palatial residence. The views from the airing courts and from the windows are most extensive and beautiful. To the south lies a broad stretch of highly cultivated country, having the bold and varied outlines of the Pentland Hills in the background to the west; other parts of Dreghorn and Bonaly with the valleys of Leith and Almond Waters in the distance; north of the poorhouse on Morningside, the Grange and other southern suburbs of the city; and on the east Arthur's Seat leads the eye farther on to the Firth of Forth and the lonely, distant line of hills beyond. From its situation, the Poorhouse, though standing high, is well sheltered from the north and northeast. The wind to which it will be chiefly exposed will be the west and it is proposed to plant a bolt of trees on Wester Craiglockhart Hill in order to moderate the breezes coming from that direction.

The principal approach to the building is from the Morningside road, about ¼ mile to the south of the Morningside toll bar. It was expected that the old church road by Greenbank Farm would be available for access to the poorhouse from Morningside, but after some litigation, this was departed from and ground was feued from

The New Poorhouse

Mr. Trotter of Mortonhall for the present new approach. The principal lodge and entrance gate are placed on the end next the Morningside public road at the boundary of the Board's property. Another new road giving access from Slateford has been formed through the valley between East and West Craiglockhart Hills. It starts from the Colinton Road near Craiglockhart Farmhouse and, passing by the side of the old tower or keep, now in ruins, rises by gentle gradient to the site of the poorhouse. A lodge has been placed on this road at the northwest boundary of the site. Various other roads required for the efficient working of the poorhouse and proper employment of inmates in agricultural labour have been formed across the fields forming the site. The new buildings and the enclosed airing courts cover an area of about 16 acres. It is proposed to devote to about 36 acres of arable ground solely for poorhouse purposes and this will be cultivated by such of the inmates as are fitted for agricultural work. West Craiglockhart Hill which joins the Poorhouse grounds will also probably be retained for poorhouse purposes and will be laid out in walks and cultivated so far as practicable by pauper labour.

The new Poorhouse faces the south and will ultimately consist of three groups of distinct buildings viz. the main Poorhouse in the centre, the infirmary to the east and the lunatic asylum to the west. At present only the Poorhouse and the Infirmary have been erected, though the site of the Lunatic Asylum has been partly excavated and levelled.

The style of the buildings is Scotch, which harmonises well with the surrounding scenery. The whole is treated in a plain and simple way without expensive or ornamental details. The architectural effect, which is pleasing, to chiefly obtained from the mass and extent of the building and by the arrangement of the plan in breaking it up into a number of separate blocks. At the centre of the main poorhouse, a corbelled tower octagonal in form rises to the height of 105 feet and a picturesque and varied outline is given to the long fronts by numerous bold projections crowned with crow stepped gables.

The main object of the Poorhouse undoubtedly is to provide a comfortable home for the deserving poor, who either through sickness or misfortune, may be deprived of adequate means of subsistence, or whose age and infirmities prevent them from supporting themselves. At the same time however, poorhouses are also intended to serve as a test of real poverty and to assist in the working of the Poor Law Act by the detection of the lazy and the vicious. To render the Poorhouse unattractive to such classes and to keep them under proper restraint when they are inmates, a harsher treatment and a sterner discipline are necessary than would be required than if the good and industrious resided within its walls. To reconcile these two opposite objects- to furnish within the same building, on the one hand, a comfortable home for the aged and the unfortunate, and on the other hand, a reformatory for the vicious, has been the great difficulty of poorhouse architects and the great trial of poorhouse officials. Possibly the ultimate solution of the problem may lie, as has been already suggested in these columns, in such a modification of the present Poor Law as may enable the two classes to be treated in separate establishments, specially designed for their respective objects. Under the present Poor Law, such a plan cannot be tried. But there is but one uniform treatment for the good and the bad, for the industrious and for the idle. Except insofar as the wisdom of the officials may temper the law in its administration. The managers of the Craiglockhart Poorhouse made an attempt to relax the existing regulations in the case of respectable married couples, by providing cottages in which they might reside together within the poorhouse walls, but they were informed by the Board of Supervision that this was illegal, and they were not allowed to put their proposal into execution.

To carry out efficiently in the working of the Poorhouse the present regulations of the Board of Supervision, it is essential that there shall be an entire separation of the various classes and that the officials shall have the power both of sub-classifying the inmates at pleasure and also of keeping them under constant surveillance. The architects Messrs. George Beattie and Sons appeared to have successfully carried out the separation of the various classes at Craiglockhart Poorhouse. The classes are entirely isolated from one another in separate blocks of buildings, each complete within itself and every class has a spacious airing courts allotted into its own use. Those for the doubtful classes are surrounded by the Poorhouse buildings and offices, while the better-behaved have airing courts facing the south,

The New Poorhouse

tastefully laid out with walks and plots in which flowers and shrubs will be cultivated.

The separation of the building into a number of detached blocks joined only at one point by a connecting corridor is a peculiarity of the Craiglockhart Poorhouse. The separate block system adopted gives facilities for ventilation and for obtaining sunlight and fresh air for the inmates. It will also permit of the total isolation of any particular class of inmates in case of an epidemic breaking out and it affords special advantages in case of fire, which, even should it gain ahead, can only destroy the block in which it originates, and it would not involve the whole building in a general conflagration.

The second peculiarity of the building are the special facilities afforded for efficient administration and for the smooth working of establishment with a small staff of officials. The Poorhouse consists of an administrative block in the centre, two blocks in line with it to the west for the male paupers, and two blocks in line with it to the east for female paupers. As the females are considerably more numerous than the males, a third block is provided for them to the north of the other two and facing eastwards. The buildings are three storeys in height, except the east wing block, which is only two stories high. The central corridor of communication which connects the various blocks on each floor is in one unbroken line from end to end, without any stepped-on difference of level, and from it the officials can both by day and by night keep a constant supervision of the various classes without requiring even to enter the wards. This corridor is six feet four inches wide and is thoroughly well lighted and ventilated directly from an external air between each block.

In the administrative block at the centre and separating the male and female portions of the building, are the offices of the Governor and Matron and the other official apartments. Immediately behind is the dining hall and beyond it the kitchen compartment and stores are concentrated in a two-storey block immediately facing the back entrance, so that all goods on their delivery are once carried into them. They are in the immediate neighbourhood of the kitchen, where so many of the articles are to be used and have also separate serving rooms attached for males and females, where articles not used in the kitchen are distributed to the parties coming for them from the wards. The kitchen, which stands between the stores and the dining hall, has also serving rooms attached to it, communicating both with the dining hall and the service passages from which the food is served out with great rapidity, either to the dining hall or the wards.

From the special arrangements adopted, none of the paupers, except those regularly employed in the kitchen and stores, can ever be there without immediate detection and thus pilfering and many other evils are avoided. From the concentration which has been effected, not only can the governor and matron keep a constant supervision over these important departments, but also a much smaller staff of paid officials will be able to do the work than could otherwise have accomplished it.

We come next to the sanitary arrangements. Each class is provided with separate water closets, lavatories, and baths upon every floor, to which they have ready access to both by night and by day. Closets are placed in projections opposite the staircase at the centre of each block and are entirely cut off from the wards by doors and intermediate lobbies, having thorough cross ventilation. The apparatus is all of a strong durable description and is not liable to get out of order from rough usage, while from its simplicity and the great amount of light and ventilation, cleanliness is ensured. In addition to the baths attached to the wards, there is also provided a general bathing establishment with dressing and undressing rooms and a dozen baths placed in one large and lofty apartment lighted from the roof and well ventilated. The paupers will be at bathed in detachments at the regular periods.

There are special arrangements for heating and ventilation. The two walls of the central corridor are built hollow and a series of chambers about three feet six inches are formed along the whole extent of the wall on both sides of the corridor. These chambers are made use of for extracting the foul air and supplying the fresh heated air. In every block two hot chambers are provided, in which fresh cold air brought from the outside of the buildings is heated by powerful coils of steam pipes and is conveyed by the hollowed chambers to the various

The New Poorhouse

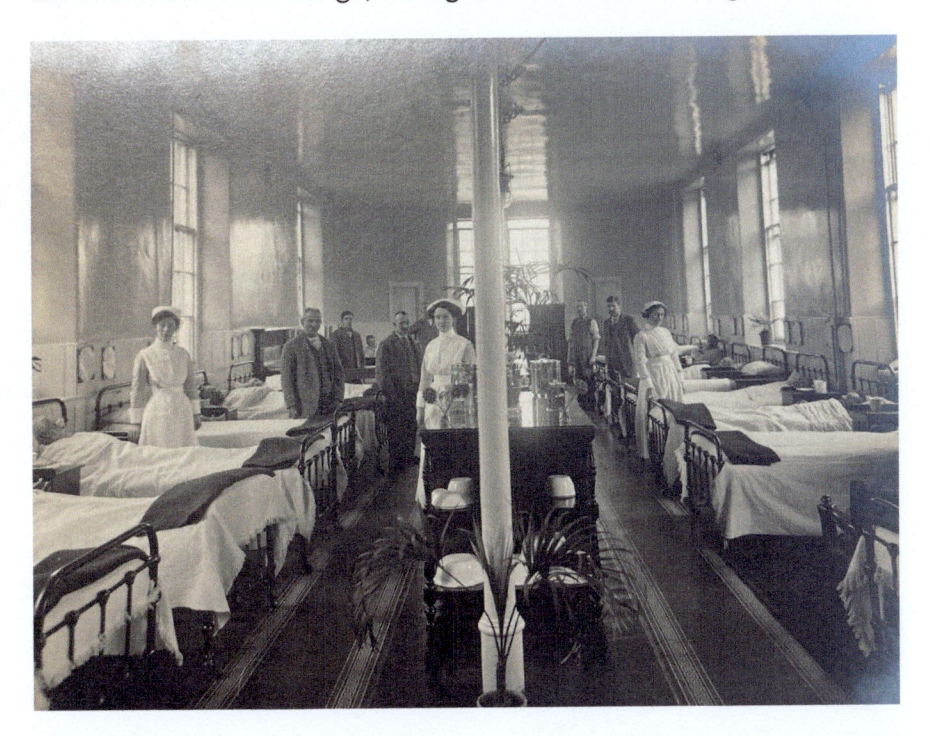

floors. For ventilation a central foul air trunk is provided in the roof of every block to and each ward has several of the chambers in the hollow walls acting as extracting flues and leading the foul air up to the central trunk. At the middle of each block, a hot chamber is formed where the foul air is rarefied by the heat from a hot water cistern, and a current being thus produced, the foul air escapes through a large ventilator into the open atmosphere. Each ward is also provided with Sheringham's patent ventilators in the external walls for the supply of fresh cold air so that a constant circulation is maintained during the night and at other times when the windows are all closed. The day rooms and dormitories for the various classes of paupers are all large and spacious apartments. They are 35 feet long by 18 feet wide and have 12 feet ceilings, giving in the dormitories the cubic airspace on the average of nearly 500 feet per bed. The wards are heated at each end by a large open fireplace with an iron grate and mantelpiece of new design, projecting boldly into the apartment, and, having fire-brick back and sides, so as to radiate heat in all directions. The fireplace openings have circular heads and spandrels on each side are ornamental with foliage, having the Poorhouse monogram and that date in low relief. The walls of the wards and the passages have been linked to the height of 4 feet 6 inches from the floor. This is a most admirable arrangement, and not only makes the rooms much more comfortable, but will prevent the constant breakage of plaster which he occurs in poorhouses. The lining on the walls and the other woodwork has been varnished and the plasterwork above size-coloured of a light-green tint. The general appearance of the walls is most pleasing and comfortable. The plasterwork of all the bathrooms, lavatories and water closets is painted in oil and the woodwork varnished. The provision for each separate class is complete in itself, with day-rooms, dormitories separate staircase and airing-courts and all the necessary sanitary conveniences.

The male paupers are divided into four classes – old men of good character, doubtful old men, dissolute men and boys, and the females into seven classes, old women of good character, married women, doubtful old women, dissolute women, girls, children under five, and infants. The various classes are disposed of in the most advantageous way, both with reference to one another and to the general working of establishment.

The dining hall is a large and handsome apartment 74 feet by 48 feet, with accommodation for dining 600 paupers. This is divided by iron columns into a centre and to side compartments, and the ceiling is panelled in squares with ornamental main couples, brackets and pendants and has a most light and elegant effect. There is a platform at one end suitable for addresses, concerts etc. and as the dining hall is at present to be used as a church for the poorhouse, the pulpit will be in the meantime placed here. The seating is all open supported on iron standards so arranged that the seats can be folded up for cleaning out the hall daily. A better poorhouse hall we will undertake to say it is not to be found in the kingdom.

The kitchen is 30 feet square by 19 feet high and is thoroughly lighted and cross ventilated by large clerestory windows on each side going right up to the ceiling, so that all steam or vitiated air can be swept away. The kitchen and the scullery adjoining are fitted up with the most powerful steam cooking apparatus. In the kitchen there are six steam cooking vessels, several of them five feet in diameter and in the scullery, there are two large steamers for vegetables, which are prepared by steam in open wire trays, much quicker and better that they could be boiled in water.

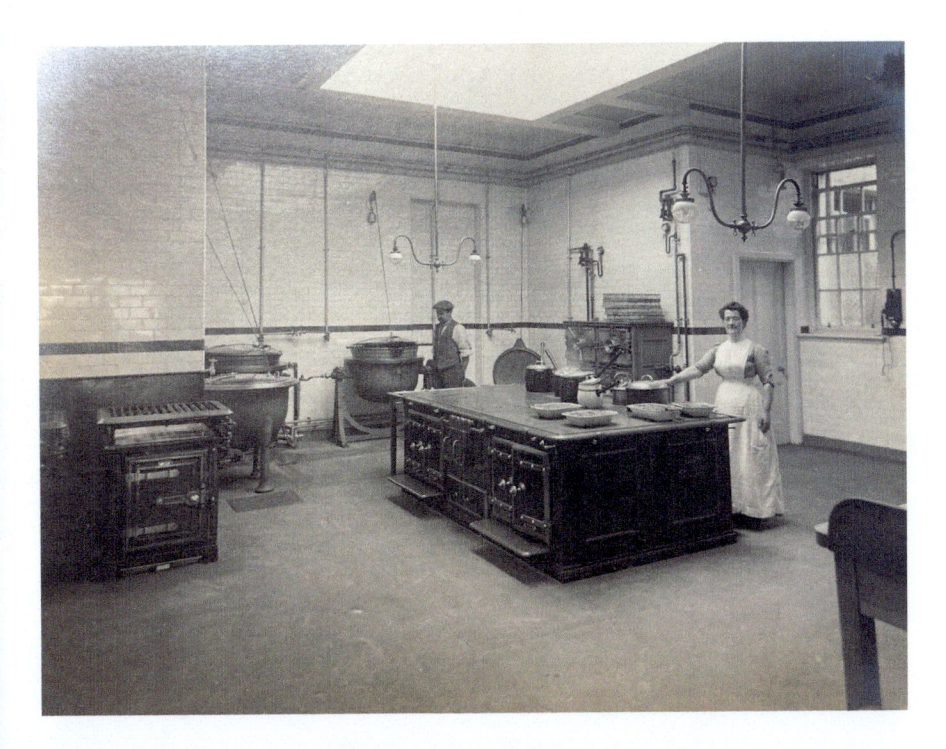

At the back of the internal female airing- courts is situated the washing department and the enclosed drying and bleaching greens. The washing department is divided into two separate establishments that for the main poorhouse and that for the infirmary and having all the appliances and apparatus in duplicate, as this was considered necessary to prevent risk of infection. The steam washing and drying apparatus is of a practicable kind, the dirty clothes being taken in at one end of the building and delivered dry and clean up the other end and in a very short space of time.

Beside the washing department are placed two powerful steam boilers, which do the whole heating and cooking of the Poorhouse and the Infirmary and also drive the steam engine which pumps up the water to the cistern in the central tower. Adjoining is a bakehouse in which can be prepared the whole bread used in the Poorhouse.

At the back of the internal male courts are the workshops for the smiths, carpenters, plumbers, tinsmiths, carpenters, tailors, shoemakers, book binders etc. and adjoining these are extensive farm offices. These embrace a farm court with stabling, byre and cart shed, implement house, piggery etc. all arranged on the most modern and improved system. Beside the back entrance gate are placed the porter's lodge and probationary wards. Here the newly arrived paupers are received and examined before being admitted into the house. Proper waiting and examination rooms, baths, lavatories, clothes stores, and disinfecting apparatus are provided here. There is also a weighing machine for checking all goods coming in.

The Infirmary is designed upon the pavilion system now universally adopted in all new hospitals. There are four pavilions arranged in pairs for ordinary cases and a fifth pavilion at the back, entirely detached, to be used exclusively as a fever hospital. At the centre of the corridor which connects the pavilions is placed the administrative block which contains the officials' apartments, the dispensary storerooms and kitchen accommodation. The pavilions are two storeys in height and contain one ward on each floor. The longer axis of the pavilions is from north to south but inclining slightly to the east, which ensures the sun shining on both sides of the wards every day in the year and protects them from the cold north east winds. The ordinary wards are 60 feet by 22 feet and the fever wards 86 feet by 23. They are lighted by large windows on both sides and at the ends and careful provision is made for their thorough ventilation at all times. Fresh air fresh cold air is supplied when the windows are closed by Sheringham's ventilators in the external walls. The wards are warmed by a large open fireplace projecting out into the apartment and radiating the heat on all sides. The grates for these fireplaces have been specially designed and have large hot chambers behind the fire, into which fresh cold air can be admitted at pleasure and after, being thoroughly heated, enters the ward at the ceiling. The lavatories and water closets are placed upon the external angles at one end of the pavilions. This position secures better than any other that thorough ventilation indispensable for these sanitary appliances and they are further cut off from the wards by intervening lobbies, well lighted and cross ventilated. And the other end of the wards are the scullery and the nurse's room. The former is fitted up with a hot and cold-water sink and from a window in the latter, the nurse can command the patients in the ward both day and night. The bathroom is placed beside the nurse's room and there is also a serving room for distributing food coming from the kitchen to the patients. The walls of the wards are lined with wood to the height of four feet six inches from the floor, varnished, and the plaster walls above and the ceilings are oil painted. This will prevent are a great extent the absorption by the walls of poisonous gases. The wards are lighted at night, in connection with which extracting flues for foul air are provided. The lobbies and staircases are heated by coils of steam pipes. Special airing grounds for the infirmary patients extend to four acres and will be laid out in grass and shrubbery, with proper walks so that that convalescent patients may at any time enjoy half an hour's exercise. To the south, the infirmary airing grounds are only enclosed by a low wall and an open iron railing. The whole infirmary has been planned and carried out on the most modern principles and for its size will be remarkably complete.

The Governor of the Poorhouse is accommodated in a detached villa erected on the ground to the west of the main building and the other officials and apartments within the house.

As the Edinburgh Water Company Act did not embrace the Poorhouse within the area of supply, it became necessary to obtain a Bill to extend the area so as to include the Poorhouse. This was passed during the last session of Parliament, but the necessary works authorised in connection with the Bill have not been begun yet. Efforts are a present being made to obtain an additional supply of water from a well on the Poorhouse site. In the centre tower of the poorhouse at a level above the roofs of the other buildings is placed a large iron cistern or tank containing nearly 20,000 gallons of water, which is distributed by gravitation to the whole establishment. This tower also contains a clock, having dials on four sides. In connection with it there is a large bell weighing upwards of 10 cwt for striking the hours. The Poorhouse buildings are lighted throughout with gas – the pipes all being iron and the brackets and pendants of the strongest and simplest description. The Edinburgh Gas Company are at present laying a large new main from Morningside to supply the Poorhouse. There are separate and independent systems of drainage for the sewerage, the rainwater from the roofs and the surface water from the airing courts and roads. The sewerage is collected in covered filtering tanks and will be made use of for agricultural purposes. The rainwater from the roofs is stored in a large tank adjoining the washing department and will be pumped up by the steam engine for washing purposes.

The total number of pauper inmates for whom accommodation is at present provided is 1000 viz. 740 in the main poorhouse and 260 in the infirmary. The lunatic asylum which, as we have said, is not yet begun will accommodate 160 additional. The contracts for the poorhouse, infirmary and governor's house at present erected amount to about 45,000 pounds, exclusive of roads and we understand there is every prospect that the whole expenditure will not exceed the sum originally contemplated viz 50,000 pounds.

The New Poorhouse

The Forres, Elgin and Nairn Gazette December 1871
Even in death...

Another matter was brought before the Board by Professor Geikie upon the question of forming a graveyard[12] at Craiglockhart Poorhouse. The conclusion of the report was that such grounds could not be formed there without imminent risk to the Craiglockhart farm and mansion-house water supply. In these circumstances it was recommended by the Law Committee either to come to an arrangement with one of the cemetery companies or that the Town Council should be called upon to provide a cemetery for the city. In the course of conversation about this recommendation, it came out that the mangers of two of our cemeteries had demurred to having anything to do with the interment of paupers, alleging that their want of success was due to the fact that hitherto they had accepted such.

---

12   Morningside cemetery opened in 1878 and many inmates were buried there in unmarked graves. Professor Geikie himself is buried alongside them.

"Comfort for the poor, care for the ratepayer"
The motto on the architectural plans for the new Poorhouse.

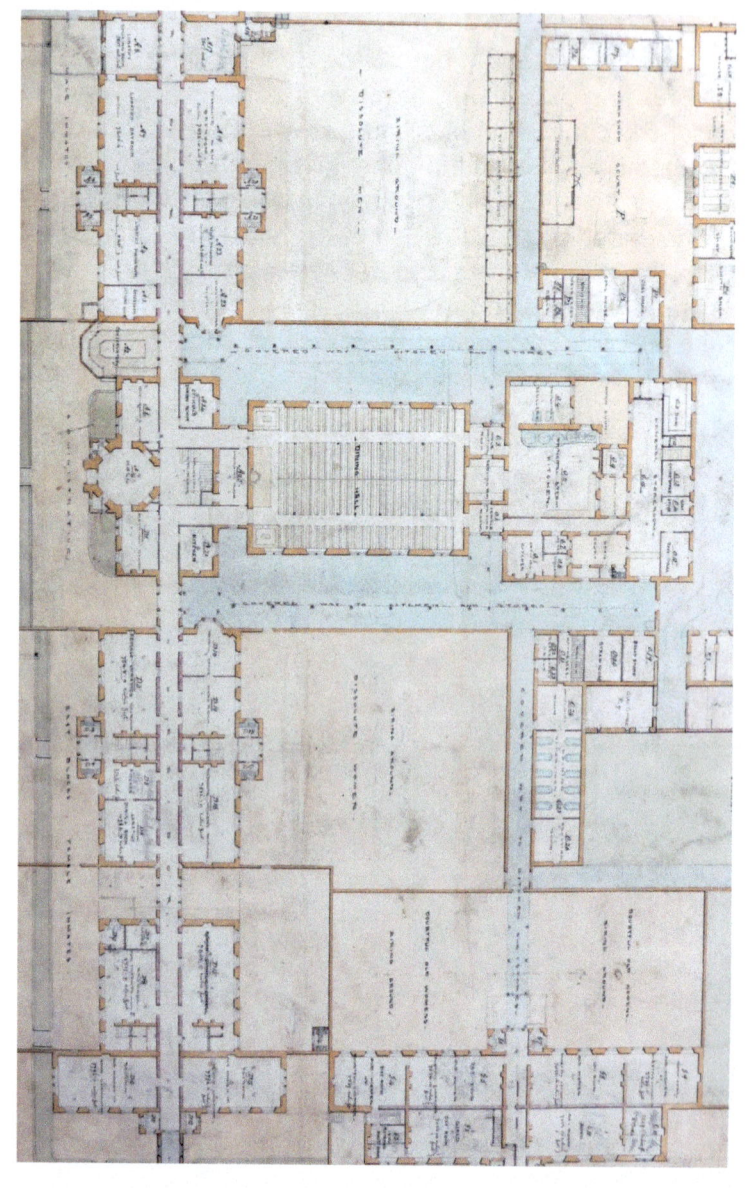

Plan of the main Poorhouse, showing an airing ground for 'Dissolute Men' and airing grounds for 'Dissolute Women' and 'Doubtful Women'.
By kind permission Edinburgh City Archives.

Chapter 4

Running the Poorhouse

The 1845 Act relieved the onus on the pauper him- or herself to establish a right of settlement in a parish, and thus entitlement to relief. This provision then led to what appear to be often hard-fought disputes between parishes as to who had the liability, often with harsh consequences. Several were recorded in the press.

The City Poorhouse, designated for the entire City of Edinburgh as one parish for the purposes of the 1845 Act, is situated within the local parish of Colinton in South West Edinburgh.

The Glasgow Herald December 1880
Parish of Colinton v. the City Parish of Edinburgh

The Parochial Board of the Parish of Colinton near Edinburgh sought in this action for declarator that they were not liable for pauper children born in the Edinburgh City Poorhouse, which is situated in the Colinton Parish. Since the erection of the City Poorhouse in 1870, it has been the custom of the defenders to send out female paupers to be confined there. An illegitimate child born in the City Poorhouse in 1872, whose mother had no Scotch residential settlement and is now dead had become chargeable to the Colinton Parish. The parochial authorities there claimed relief in this action and the question came to be whether or not Colinton Parish is to be held liable for relief to all pauper children born in the City Poorhouse, the mothers being sent there from the Edinburgh City Parish purposely to be confined,

The City Parochial Board maintained that Colinton was liable, in respect that they had been regularly assessed for poor rates as owners and occupiers of the Poorhouse and lands in the parish of Colinton and had paid during such occupancy for upwards of £597.

The question was recently debated and today the Lord Ordinary has issued an interlocutor finding that the settlement of the pauper must be held to be in the Parish of Colinton where he was born. The theory of the pursuer that the Poorhouses is constructively in the Parish of Edinburgh was not, his Lordship said, supported by any authority whatever. If it were to be entertained at all, it would seem to follow than it should hold good for all parochial purposes, but the parish of Colinton did not so extend it, as was seen in the levying of the poor rates.

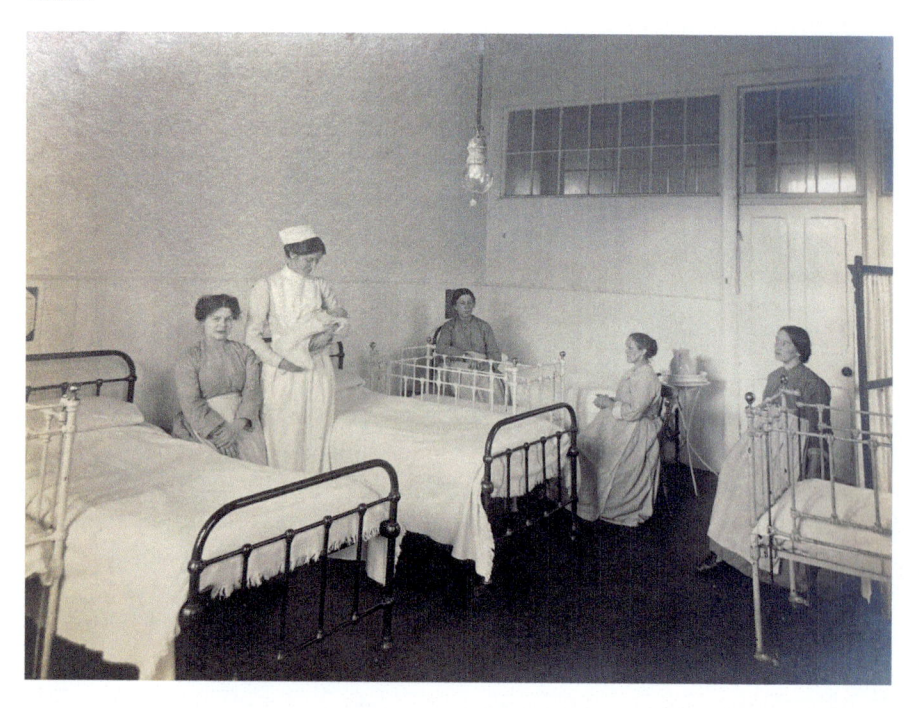

Edinburgh Evening News February 1876
The children born in Craiglockhart Poorhouse.

At the Colinton Parochial Board meeting on Saturday, the dispute with the City of Edinburgh Board as to the maintenance of the children born in Craiglockhart Poorhouse was discussed. The committee appointed to consider the question of the liability of the parish recommended that the Board should resist all claims for these children made by the City of Edinburgh Parochial Board, leaving the City Board to take its own course, the committee being satisfied that the question would have to be determined judicially. Mr Greig, Inspector of the City Parish, believed that the City Parish would willingly take all the responsibility of the children born in the Craiglockhart Poorhouse, provided the Colinton Board departed from the claims for poor rates for the house. He pointed out there was a decision in the Court of Session bearing on the case at issue. It was found that the City Parish was liable for the children born in the Maternity Hospital, Minto House, although the mothers had simply been sent from Saint Cuthbert's Parish to the hospital to be confined. Colinton derived £300 a year as poor rates from the City Parish and all the burdens from the City Poorhouse which they had had to bear amounted to £15. The report of the committee was adopted, Mr Greig dissenting.

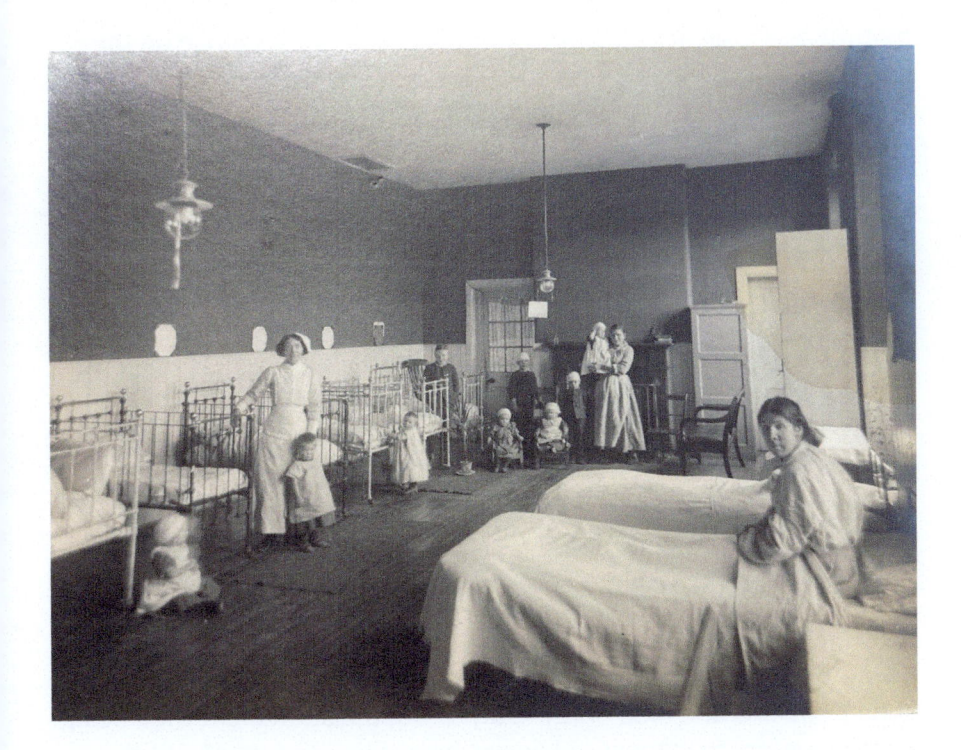

The Banffshire Reporter January 1874
A curious Poor Law case

A correspondent writes- about a dozen years ago, a young painter named MacPherson left Tain for the South and it appears that some time ago he married an Edinburgh widow who had five children under 12 years of age and on the poor roll. The painter and widow quarrelled. He was put in prison for assault, and she and her children went into the poorhouse in Edinburgh, where she died two days after being admitted. What has become of McPherson nobody can tell: but the curious result of this unfortunate matrimonial business is that the five young paupers were kept in the Edinburgh Poorhouse at the expense of the Parish of Tain, as the birthplace of the husband of the late mother, until an enormous account was run up against the Parochial Board of Tain. There was some talk of going to law, but Parochial Boards are generally sick of going to law and it is said that there is a similar case on record, throwing the expense on the birth parish of the person marrying widow. The five pauper children are now be taken to the Easter Ross Union. Supposing the man who was the means of throwing them on the Union to have died or gone abroad, what connections can these children be supposed out with a parish of Tain? With plenty of tramps, a number of widows and orphans and the proverbial easy Scottish marriage law, the settlement of young paupers may become a very tartan sort of business.

The Dalkeith Advertiser July 1918
Dalkeith Poor Law Arbitration Case

The Local Government Board have given their decision in a case, Edinburgh Parish Council vs Dalkeith Parish Council and Athelstaneford Parish Council, which was submitted to arbitration.

The facts of the case were: – Elizabeth Cairns, who was illegitimate, was born in Dalkeith on the 29th of January 1902. Her mother Bridget Cairns married Peter Logan (not the child's father) at Dalkeith on 20th June 1902 and she died on 29th July 1905, the settlement then being Athelstaneford in respect of Logan's birth. On 27th August 1908, the Society for the Prevention of Cruelty to Children sent the child from their Haddington branch to Quarriers Home, Bridge of Weir, where she remained till 10th November 1916, when she was returned to the Society for the Prevention of Cruelty to Children shelter in Edinburgh. On 14th December 1916, the Children's Shelter applied to the Edinburgh Parish Council to have her examined under the Mental Deficiency Act, but as she was under 16 years of age, this was referred to the Edinburgh School Board, as the local authority in the first instance. On 12th January 1917, the School Board replied that, though defective, she was educable and would be received into their Duncan Street school. This was intimated to Miss Hepburn of the Children's Shelter, who then applied for the girl's removal under the poor laws. Accordingly, on 23rd February 1917 Elizabeth Cairns was sent to Craiglockhart Poorhouse.

Edinburgh claimed on Dalkeith, but Dalkeith denied liability, in respect that the pauper Elizabeth Cairns was a congenital imbecile and as such must be regarded as a perpetual pupil. She could not therefore be held to be forisfamiliated (*Scots legal term meaning legally independent from parents*) at the age of 12 years, when she attained the age of puberty and accordingly, when she became chargeable to Edinburgh on 23rd February 1917, she took the settlement which her mother possessed at the time of her death on 29th July 1905 viz. the birth parish of Peter Logan, to whom her mother was married on 20 June 1902.

Athelstaneford also denied liability in respect that, being an illegitimate orphan above the age of 12 years at the date of her chargeability to Edinburgh in February 1917, Elizabeth Cairns did not take the birth settlement of her mother's husband; that mean time she had been maintained without parish aid or common begging; that not having resided continuously for three years in any parish since attaining to puberty, a settlement is in the parish of her own birth; that she was not an idiot but was certified by the medical officer of Edinburgh School Board to be educable and of a capacity to benefit by instruction in the Duncan Street Special School, and that the institution generally succeeded in enabling all their pupils to ultimately earn their own living.

In support of Dalkeith's contention, a report by Doctor Ballantyne regarding Elizabeth Cairns was produced, from which the following is an extract (There were clearly no qualms about disclosing personal medical reports in the local paper!)

Her bodily health is good though the growth is somewhat backward, and she is stunted and short for her age. As regards her mental condition, her mental powers are distinctly weak, in fact she is feeble-minded and would be classed as an imbecile. She can read and write a little but only with difficulty and very slowly. She is usually dull and silent and hardly ever speaks to anyone. I should not think it would be possible to educate her any more nor will she ever be any use at any kind of work.

The Local Government Board have issued the following determination:

The Board are of opinion that Dalkeith Parish Council are liable for the relief of the above named mentally defective pauper. Elizabeth Cairns was born in Dalkeith on 29th January 1902, being the illegitimate child of Bridget Cairns, who subsequently married and who died on 29th July 1905. As the decision in this case turns on the degree of mental incapacity of the pauper, the Board consulted the General Board of Control and have received the following report dated 18th April 1918 by Doctor Carswell viz.

I visited and examined the girl today at Craiglockhart Poorhouse. She is mentally defective, and I would class her as feeble-minded, as defined by the Mental Deficiency Act 1913. She is not insane, and she has never been certified under either the Lunacy Acts or the Mental Deficiency Act. She can read a little, write very well and she can do simple sums in arithmetic. She can give a fairly intelligent account of herself, and she can express her wishes quite rationally. She does not desire to remain where she is, nor does she desire to go back to Bridge of Weir but, although she cannot say precisely what she would like to do, she thinks she would like to be like other girls and do something for herself. The Matron told me that she did some work in the laundry, but that she required supervision as she was given to restlessness and to leading others into mischief. She looks an impulsive girl, and I can fancy that she may be difficult to control. I consider that her mental defect is not such as to prevent her from becoming forisfamiliated.

In view of Doctor Carswell's report, the Board are of opinion that Elizabeth Cairns was forisfamiliated on 29th January 1914, when she attained the age of 12 years. She then started life with her own birth settlement viz. Dalkeith. When she became chargeable in Edinburgh in February 1915, she had not resided sufficiently long in one parish to acquire a residential settlement, and accordingly a settlement is still in Dalkeith. The Board therefore hold Dalkeith Parish Council liable to relieve Edinburgh of the expenses of the chargeability.

North British Daily Mail December 1879
Parochial inhumanity

Sir – today I left Edinburgh by of the 3:05 pm train for Glasgow. Ere the train started it was my lot to see such a scene as never met my eyes since I began travelling 30 years ago. On common trolley there lay awaiting the train an old, withered creature, 84 years of age – a poor pauper being removed from an Edinburgh poorhouse to some other poorhouse in Glasgow. The spectators were horrified at such an exhibition of parochial inhumanity – a disgrace to our civilisation.

Surely even parochial red tapeism might have allowed this poor old woman to die in peace in the Edinburgh poorhouse? A probability is that this inhuman removal will hasten the poor body's demise. Is no one responsible?

I am etc. 'The Traveller'

Newry Reporter August 1907
Appeal against removal to Newry

The Local Government Board for Scotland intimated that they had dismissed the Guardian's appeal against the proposed removal of a native of Newry, named Edward Farrell, from the Craiglockhart Poorhouse in the parish of Edinburgh to the Newry Union Workhouse. They found that the appeal was incompetent, in respect that the pauper had not resided for one year within the parish of Edinburgh before applying for relief. The clerk said that this was the case which had formed the subject of a question in parliament by Mister J. McVeigh MP. Farrell, who was 75 years of age and unmarried, had spent his life in Scotland since a boy and now when he was past work, he was to be maintained at the expense of the ratepayers in the Newry Union.

The Evening Post April 1903
Leslie Parish Council

The monthly meeting of the council was held on Monday evening. In the absence of the Chairman Mr. Henry Archibald presided. The inspector's report showed that since last meeting a lunatic pauper aged 73 years then died in the asylum after being in at institution for upwards of 30 years. Leslie was found to be liable for the maintenance by a decision in the Court of Session. Among the new applications the most interesting was that of a claim from the Inspector of Poor for Edinburgh for a man at present in Craiglockhart Poorhouse who had been resident in France for 43 years and had recently got back to this country. The claim is founded on his statement of having been born in Prinlaws (near Kirkcaldy in Fife)

The Glasgow Herald August 1877
Edinburgh Parish Council

The Inspector, in reporting upon the number of inmates in the Poorhouse, remarked that the applicants for outdoor relief were very numerous, and mostly tramps. Many came from Glasgow and Dundee to get into the Edinburgh Poorhouse, because of its superior comforts and they had had complaints on that score, as persons had come from Glasgow and Dundee to get into Craiglockhart and on being refused, the towns from which they came had to pay for their return journey.

Mr. Lees moved that arrangement should be made to obtain the Ministers of Edinburgh in town to hold a fortnightly service at the Poorhouse. He said he had reason to know such a service would be highly appreciated by the inmates, the motion was not seconded. The Rev. Mr. Hannan moved that the Board should defray the expenses of the Roman Catholic clergyman who attended the poorhouse. Mr. Lewis said the motion opened a wide question. If it was passed, they would have the Episcopalians, United Presbyterian and other sects making similar claims. Other members objected that the Board had not had time to consider the motion, notice having only been given at the beginning of the meeting. Mr. Hannan intimated he would bring it up again at the next meeting (see Chapter 8).

The Falkirk Herald and Linlithgow Journal February 1876
Boarding out of pauper children

In the fourth annual report of the National Committee for the Boarding out of Pauper Children, it is stated that a review of the year 1875 indicates the steady and continuous extension of the boarding out system throughout the kingdom. From a Parliamentary return obtained during the year it appears that the number of children boarded out in cottages in England and Wales has increased. The increase having mainly taken place during the four years advocacy of the Committee. Alluding to the economic advantages of the system, a letter was quoted from the Governor of the Edinburgh Poorhouse, in which he states that four Scotch children can be comfortably boarded out for about the cost of one child in several of the London "District Schools". The committee have made many efforts and with some success to enlist the cooperation of the clergy in their objects and they had stated the investigations elicited from various parts of the kingdom refutations of the objects raised against the system by Mr. Tufnell and other officials of the central board.

The North British Agriculturalist January 1871
Removal of lunatic paupers

The regular monthly meeting of the members of the City Parochial Board was held on Monday. The minutes of the meeting of the 19th ult. were read and then those of committee meetings held since that date. A short discussion took place regarding the increasing the number of paupers during December. There were 779 poor people in the house as compared with 748 in November. The principal reason appeared to be the state of the weather. A letter was then read from the Board of Supervision in reply to an application for permission to remove about 80 lunatic paupers from the eastern division of the old City Poorhouse to Craiglockhart Poorhouse. The Board of Supervision refused to comply with a request, on the ground that the Craiglockhart Poorhouse was to present the best arranged and the most minutely classified house in Scotland and presumably the introduction of these lunatics would have had destroyed the arrangements. The paupers will therefore remain where they are for some time, after which it is expected they will be removed to Morningside Asylum. The next business was employment of a medical officer of the South Eastern district of the city. Considerable discussion took place regarding the respected qualifications of the gentlemen concerned. On the vote being taken Dr. Furley was elected by a majority of two.

Edinburgh Evening News February 1898
Edinburgh Parish Council and pauper lunatics

A special meeting of Edinburgh Parish Council was held in the Parish Council Chambers Edinburgh today – Mr. Clark presiding.

The Chairman called attention to a paragraph in the report of the managers of the Edinburgh Royal Asylum with regard to the accommodation of pauper lunatics, it being stated that, keeping in view the removal of a number of pauper lunatics and the proportionately heavier charge against those who remained, the managers had reluctantly come to the conclusion that they must increase the rate by £1 yearly. He thought it was unfair of the asylum managers to bring this upon them in the way it had been done, considering what the Council had done for them. The managers asked the Council to remove some of their patients as soon as possible and this was done at very great inconvenience. The Council spent £4500 making arrangements in their Craiglockhart Poorhouse and, without a word of intention of anything taking place, the managers came forward to penalise them. He thought a protest should be made that the meeting of the asylum authorities. Mr. McLaren said that taking into account the urgent way the managers pushed the council to take away certain patients, this was most unfair treatment. Not only did the managers tie the Council down to a date, but they enforced the removal of 60 patients before the council was ready to take them away. He was prepared to move that they refuse the extra £1. Mr. Forbes Dallas pointed out in one portion of the manager's report, they stated that they had obtained great advantage from the removal by the Parish Council of a number of their patients. The must be some want of memory about the whole negotiations connected with this agreement. During the negotiations, the case of their patients was discussed over and over again and there was not the smallest indication that they dreamed of increasing the charge. Mr. Stalker said the managers, in the springing this mine upon them, had broken their honour. The matter was sent to the Chairman's Committee for report.

East Aberdeenshire Observer January 1888
The case for women on Parochial Boards.

The meeting of the Parochial Board on Tuesday night does not seem to have been a very harmonious one. That scene where one of the members was speaking to Forbes' complaints and apparently, rather the speaking on his behalf, the others stamped their feet and silenced him, is to some extent inexplicable. People, like the writer, who may not know much about the working of Boards, would think that the fullest information on all matters in connection with the management is most desirable. Perhaps they might be improved by the introduction of a few ladies. The fact that there are three ladies on the Edinburgh Poorhouse Board gave Professor Blackie a text for one of his characteristically comic speeches the other night and his remarks might not have some inaptness to Peterhead. He began by saying that he would like to hear anyone with courage enough to say to that women should not be members of Parochial Boards. The whole progress of civilisation and the work of Christianity showed he said that the elevation of women stood foremost in public progress. Not that he wished by any means to confront that which God made different. He (the professor) hated what his father used to call a" he woman". He would not even look at her, and he didn't like to sit beside her. God made men and women for different purposes. They were as different as the oak tree from the birch tree – although both are trees – or as one flower from another. But it was quite certain that, wherever love and pity and kindly interest and a superior power of moral fragrance were wanted, there women should always be. In short, he thought men were utterly unfit for attending to many things of that kind, both on the Education and Poor Boards, for women had a heart to feel and an eye to see when men were hard and blind. Suppose a woman had been on the Visiting Committee of the Peterhead Poorhouse, a would not the filthy condition of the beds have been earlier discovered?

The Scotsman July 1907
Conditions at Craiglockhart

Mr. White moved that it be remitted to the House Committee to inquire and report as to the accuracy of the statements made by an ex-pauper regarding Craiglockhart Poorhouse and published in the *Dispatch* newspaper, and credited by that stage well as being truthful, straightforward and honest. Some grave charges, he said, had been made and, if not true, should not be allowed to stand. The Council had been pressed very severely by the Trades Council, who made charges, which they knew were not true. He thought the House Committee should prepare a statement and give it to the newspapers. Mr. Welsh, who seconded, said the Council had nothing to be ashamed of. The Chairman thought they should let the matter die away. If the Council did anything, they would be simply exalting the ex-pauper to a position he was dying to attain. They should let the matter fall and be done with it. Mr. White said the article said had some effect on the members and officials. A man and his wife at Craiglockhart had sent in their resignations. He would not have taken the matter up, had not the *Dispatch* stated in a leader that the articles were straightforward, truthful and honest. However, if the members did not wish him to press the matter, he was quite agreeable to drop his motion. It was unanimously agreed to let the matter drop.

The committee was appointed to inquire into the conditions of labour at the poorhouses and to report. In view of a complaint against the gatekeepers at Craiglockhart Poorhouse, the House Committee reported that there was no evidence that the gatekeeper or his wife had been disrespectful. Intimation was made of the resignation of Dr. Robertson, resident medical officer at Craiglockhart. The Chairman said she had done a lot of good work and she carried the good wishes of the Council with her. (Applause). It was agreed that in filling the position a male doctor should be appointed. Consequent upon a letter from the Edinburgh District Trades Council, it was remitted to the House Committee to consider the advisability of inserting a 'fair wages' clause into the Council contracts.

The Midlothian Journal December 1904
The work of the Parish Council

The Chairman gave a short statement as to what the Council was doing and also with reference to the condition of pauperism in Edinburgh. The parish had during the past half-year 4861 applications, and of these 1640 were admitted to Craiglockhart Poorhouse and 1555 per were admitted to Craigleith – all together an increase of 712. There had been 574 claims made against other parishes. The number of people getting outdoor relief in May 1904 was 1783. In November 1904, the number was 1852, showing an increase of 69. The number of poor chargeable to the parish at 15th November 1903 was 1718. The number of ordinary inmates in the poorhouses as at May 1904 was 1236, against 1320 in November this year, an increase of 84 on the six months. While, as compared with a corresponding period of last year, the increase was 32. The number of children at board on 15th May 1904 was 568 and at November 573, or an increase of five, and compared with the corresponding period last year, there was an increase of 13. The number of lunatics chargeable at 15th May was for 1104 and at 15th November 1128 and the number a year ago was 1111. Altogether they had boarded in asylums 843 lunatics and of these, 256 were in the Royal Edinburgh Asylum, as against 410 on 15th May last: 198 in the Edinburgh District Asylum at Bangour: 157 at Craiglockhart: and 65 at Middleton Hall. With relatives and in private dwellings they had boarded out 285 patients. It was, he though, very satisfactory to know that they were in a position to house 420 of these people in their own asylums and that, with the 423 in other asylums, they had a total of 843 under their administration. In that total he was not including the 285 boarded out with relatives and in private asylums, and these could not be regarded as acute cases of lunacy. Figures indicated to them that the sooner they can complete the Bangour Asylum and have all their patients in their own houses, the better it would it be for the whole community. During the half year, the relieving committees had done most excellent work. They had 66 meetings and disposed of 8840 cases, 1271 of which were new cases and 7569 old cases reconsidered.

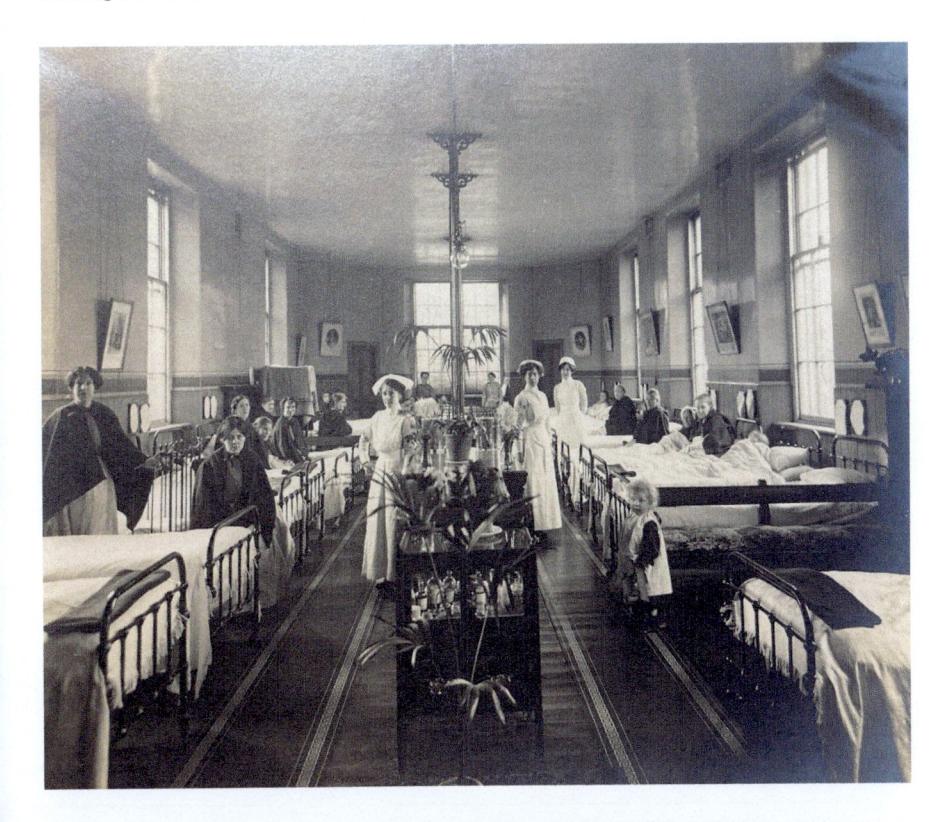

Caring for the children

One very important feature of that part of their work was that they had been able to feed a large number of children, who were on the outdoor roll. Is just about a year since that matter was discussed, and it was remitted to the relieving committee and had been carried out by them with the very greatest success. The scheme was inaugurated in the beginning of June and since that date, 400 children had been placed upon the food register. Some of these were now working, and others were off the roll of the parish. And present 346 children were receiving food six days of the week, and since the commencement, 20,627 dinners been given in restaurants all over the city, the cost for these being 1½d each, or £128 pounds 18 shillings and four pence. 34 schools were supplied with tickets every week, and 18 restaurants provided the food, which was good and varied. The headmasters and mistresses had all along been greatly interested in the scheme and had favourably commented upon it. The plan had proved a distinct success, and it was worthy of note that Edinburgh was the first Parish Council to adopt such a scheme, and he thought they could congratulate themselves on having led the way in this work, which was doing so much to benefit these poor children. He might say that Mr. Ferrier, their clerk, had been asked as to their mode and system of carrying out the scheme by many Parish Councils in the country. During the present winter to 1025 pairs of boots and 2050 pairs of stockings had been granted to children on the outdoor roll attending school.

The Mid Lothian Journal January 1908
"The ins and outs"
What Edinburgh proposes to do

The problem of the "Ins and outs"- those paupers who make it a practice of visiting the Poorhouse periodically – has been long one of some difficulty for parish councillors to solve. Edinburgh Parish Council have taken steps to consider the matter, and the report was submitted to Monday's meeting of the Council. It was to the effect that the subcommittee, having carefully considered the remit from the Ins and outs Committee of 12 Inst. to inquire and report as to what accommodation can be obtained at the Poorhouse for test purposes; also, to consider the question of a dietary and rules and regulations, and having visited both poorhouses and consulted with governors, agreed to submit the following, as to their report under the remit:

Accommodation – Males

At Craiglockhart Poorhouse there are six sheds constructed of wood, which were formerly occupied by the test class, but had not been used for test purposes for a number of years. These sheds are built close up to the west wall of the existing shoemaker's shop and this building can easily be converted by removing a partition wall the end and chimneys betwixt the shoemakers shop and passage; and the room, at present used as a cutting room, can be extended in a similar manner, for use as the labour-master's room. The building should be heated by a stove, and ingress and egress obtained by a door formed through one of the test sheds into the dining room. In front of the sheds close, boarding of a suitable height should be erected, allowing sufficient space for a passage there. Suitable lavatory accommodation can be provided, and arrangements made for allowing the men to the open air at stated periods when off work. The shoemakers' department can be transferred to the granary adjoining, access being obtained by an outside stair, and granary removed to a position over stables.

At Craigleith Poorhouse there are eight sheds of brick construction which were built for test cases, but which have not been used for such for several years. The sheds are situated in an airing yard at the northwest wing of the poorhouse, and the male sleeping ward numbered 368 on the ground floor convenient to the sheds can be used as a dining room, day room and dormitory. Close boarded partition eight feet high should be erected in front of the sheds, allowing a passage six feet wide, and the cemented area at the northwest corner of the ward, so can be used as an airing yard. The openings in existing railing surrounding this area should be closed and the railing itself raised to a height of seven feet six inches, with a barbed wire fixed on top. Direct access to the test sheds from the dining room to can be obtained by forming one of the end windows into a door, and arrangements can be made for lavatory purposes by utilising one of the test sheds. There will be provision in all for seven men, which the governor considers ample, but the above ward will not be available until the governor's present house is free for use as dormitories.

The subcommittee, in suggesting these arrangements, have kept in view as far as possible, the complete isolation and separation of the class of paupers proposed to be dealt with, from the ordinary inmates of the poorhouses.

Rules and regulations for the test class.

1. The persons, hereinafter described as the test class, should be housed in a department of each poorhouse to be specially arranged and isolated from all other portions of the poorhouse and they shall be confined by lock and key. They shall be under the frequent supervision of the labour-master, who shall sleep in a portion of the said special department.
2. The test department shall consist firstly of sheds, wherein they shall work separately by day, at such work as the medical officer shall think suitable; secondly of a room wherein they may all sleep at night, take their meals by day and remain after work hours, or all day, if not considered in a fit state of health to work in the sheds.
3. The meals shall be served in the common room at the usual meal hours of the poorhouse and shall conform to all the ordinary poor house rules as to hours of rising etc.
4. These inmates shall attend worship in the hall but shall be marched there and back in charge of the labour-master and shall be seated apart from the other inmates.
5. They shall be supplied with the Class B diet, but stone breakers who break six cwt of whin metal, oakum teasers who tease 2lbs of rope and bundlers of firewood who make up 300 bundles per day will receive diet Class C.
6. They shall, under no circumstances, be allowed to leave the Poorhouse on leave of absence and shall never be employed by the governor on work outside the Poorhouse precincts.
7. They shall be allowed no tobacco or snuff.
8. They shall never be allowed to attend any entertainment that may be given in the Poorhouse, nor be allowed to share in the special diet that may be given to other inmates on any special occasion.

9. They should be obliged to keep their apartments clean, to the satisfaction of the governors and the labour-master and they shall also clean the labour-master's apartment.
10. The furniture of the common room shall consist of the ordinary furniture used in the poorhouses.
11. The foregoing rules shall apply to females to such extent as circumstances will permit.

The John O'Groats Journal, November 1882
The cold hand of charity

An old woman aged 85, who alleges she has seen better days, is at present going the round of Edinburgh. It is being suggested to her that she should go into the workhouse, at which she replied that the adviser did not know what it was. The breakfast, she alleged, in Craiglockhart Poorhouse, consisted of a cup of tea and slice of dry bread. The tea was "not tea, it was coloured" and are "made up of one half of carbonate of soda" – this is a common device for infusing purposes. Then she had a mutchkin of broth for dinner, without any meat and some other portion for afternoon service. She evidently preferred the roaming life to that of the big house and parochial nutriment. We have no means of knowing whether or not her statements are true, without going out and making enquiry. One of her complaints related to the excessive sourness of the kirn milk. It is, in any circumstances, a bitter draught that which comes from the cold hand of charity and we hope that the "skilley" is both thicker and better that the old wife alleges, or it must be bad enough. We give the reports from what it is worth and can only say that it is evidently a part of one side of a big question It is something new however to learn that they get "fatherless kail" (curly kale) in the workhouse.

Edinburgh Evening News October 1897
A bowling green but no electric lights

At a meeting of Edinburgh Parish Council, it was remitted to Messrs Stoker and Dunlop to confer with the Governor of Craiglockhart Poorhouse to obtain an estimate regarding the laying out of a Bowling Green there for the amusement of the lunatic patients. The chairman's committee unanimously agreed to recommend the council that it was inadvisable to fit up electric light in the poorhouses and in the Chambers at Castle Terrace. Mr Arnold moved on Mr Dallas seconded that this matter should be remitted to the committee to ascertain exactly what the cost of the change would be. This was agreed to by 12 votes to four. There seemed to be a desire that the Chambers at least should be lit by electricity.

Edinburgh Evening News July 1926
Something for nothing
Why Edinburgh's poorhouse is popular.

The report submitted by Mr. William Young[13], Governor of Craiglockhart Poorhouse, to yesterday's meeting of Edinburgh Parish Council showed that 837 men, whose ages ranged from 20 to 45 had been admitted to the institution during the past year. Some of these had at one time enjoyed the benefits of outdoor relief, but instead of it being an incentive to them to try and find work, it had had the opposite effect and today they did not see the necessity of looking for work when they can get something for nothing. And the only solution that he could see was some place like a labour colony, with detention for a period and where they could be brought to useful work if necessary.

The Mid Lothian Journal February 1899
Edinburgh Parish Council
Separating married couples

There is evidently a standing joke amongst the members of the Parish Council about the attendance of councillors at committee meetings. Mr. Elliott and Mr. McLaren afterwards referred to the subject by way of chaffing Mr. Hendry. The former had a grievance against committee being summoned so frequently and the latter referred to a full attendance of members at the Relieving Committee meeting over which he presided. Amongst the other preliminaries were a notice

---

13 Mr Young was Governor for many years. He appears in the press from 1917, when he sought to be exempted from call-up to the Front in WWI (see Ch 11) to 1931, when jailed for embezzlement (see Ch 7)

of motion given in by Mr. Thompson that "married couples who may be compelled to go into the poorhouse be not separated unless so desired by themselves" and an intimation by the chairman that he had a note on Mr. Stalker's behalf stating that he was more hopeful that morning. Mr. Clark hoped to see him soon amongst them again.

Paying a solicitor six shillings

Mr. Hendry took strong exception to the payment of six shillings to a solicitor for the upkeep of a child. Mr. Moffatt explained that there was no legal liability upon the man to support the child, which was not his own, but his wife's before their marriage. Previously the child was boarded out at eight shillings and sixpence per week and the solicitor offered to take the child for six shillings. The committee thought it was more economical to agree to that arrangement. In spite of this explanation, Mr. Hendry persisted in his objection, and he received the backing of his colleague Mr. Young. Mr. Hendry's scheme was to adopt the procedure followed in the case of a deserted wife and offer the poorhouse. Mr. Young laid great stress upon the fact of the ratepayers of Edinburgh being called upon to pay six shillings to a man in the position of a solicitor and did not think much of the man who had so little respect for his wife as to allow that to be done. An interjection about the man being poor did not alter Mr. Young's views, and Mr. Elliot described the course pursued as punishing mother and child. Dr. Ritchie asked if there was anything against the mother and, the reply being in the negative, he reminded the Council that it was with her they had to deal. An overwhelming majority approved of the committee's action, and Mr. Hendry smiled over in the direction of the reporters and said that he was satisfied now the matter had got into the papers. There were signs of disapproval at the expression of such an underlying motive, in the midst of which the next business was intimated by the Chairman.

Anonymous letters

A lengthy discussion took place over the subject of ovens to be introduced into Craiglockhart, the contractor having suggested certain alterations on the specifications the only point of interest involved being that doing away with a chimney stack. Mr. Welsh gave his opinion in favour or proceeding with the work and animadverted upon the contractor sending "anonymous" – he meant something else – "gratuitous", possibly, letters of advice to the committee and reminded the council that doctors differed as a reason for them not laying much stress upon the opinions given expression to in the letter. Whatever certainly existed in the mind of Mr. Welsh regarding the subject, the letter had evidently impressed Mr. Johnson and others with a desire for reconsideration and the Chairman got the matter sent back to the committee for settlement.

Denied Last Rites

The House Committee reported upon a grievance that Mr. Young had brought under notice, the circumstances of which were then David Laidlaw, an inmate of Craiglockhart Poorhouse, died there recently. The man, being a Roman Catholic, should have had previous to his death the services of a priest: but notwithstanding the fact that both patient and his friends desired this, the request was refused by the officials. Mrs. Laidlaw on the subject maintained that her husband was of the Roman Catholic faith and that he was refused the attendance of the priest. Mr. Bennett the governor's statement was that Laidlaw on the day of his admission to the Poorhouse informed the officials that he was a Protestant. He did not ask for the services of a priest and positively refused to allow a priest to be sent for, although pressed by his wife, and on the morning of his death the priest passed through the ward are more than one occasion, but he expressed no desire to speak to him.

Mr Young was not satisfied with this report and he wanted the subject remitted to a small committee of investigation, but Mr. Welsh moved the approval of the report as he could quite easily see that if the woman was sitting beside her husband nagging at him to have a priest, he might in a way consent to his being sent for. Mr. Moffatt said after they had heard the explanation of the Governor, he considered it unnecessary to make formal investigation. The Chairman was sarcastic in his summing up and in his reminiscences of another inquiry had he had made, turned out a perfect farce. He thought these investigations should not take place unless for very strong reasons and said it expressed the opinion that it was not dignified for the council to go further when Mr. Bennett had made such a direct statement, in which the nurses no doubt would support him. A remark by Mr. Young, that if they did not make enquiry, the Canon Grady had the alternative of appealing to the Local Government Board drew from the Chairman the retort that that did not frighten the Council and Canon Grady could do as he pleased. There was considerable majority against further investigation.

Asylum

The Chairman moved the appointment of Mr. Campbell Irons to the Morningside Asylum Board in room of Mr. Storey, who had resigned, and commented upon the necessity of having a man who could look upon the question with a legal mind. Recently, he said, the patients at Morningside had their board at £1.00, which meant £350 pounds to the Parish Council. There was no doubt overcrowding in the Royal Asylum and they required to remove 60 inmates to board elsewhere. He believed the Hartwood Asylum would take certain number and Stirling was also to take several. It was very likely that the question of raising the board would be raised there.

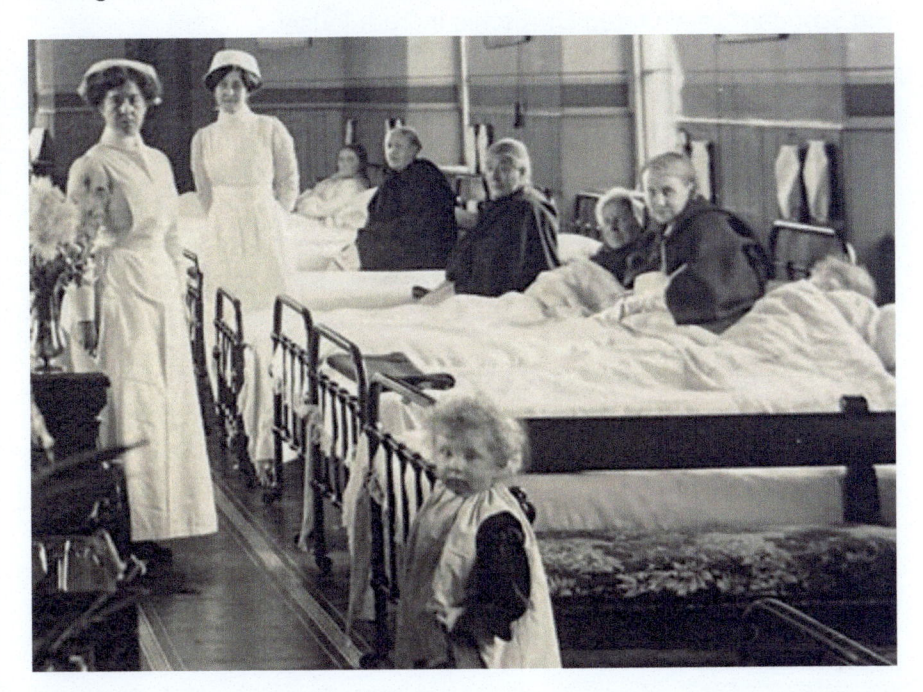

Different views on vaccination

It never does to be too sure of anything. The circular from Aberdeen Parish Council asking cooperation in a crusade to induce the Government to extend the powers of the English Vaccination Act to Scotland was read and Dr. Ritchie, who was perfect clear on the matter of vaccination being a benefit and was supported in his views by cordial "Hear, hears" from Dr Wilson, moved that it lie on the table. The Dr. was evidently labouring under the impression that such would be regarded as ungracious by Aberdeen Council and suggested a milder method, but Mr. Irons said if the Doctor moved that they decline to agree the proposal, which he believed was the unanimous feeling of the members, and then the mistaken views of Mr Irons as to unanimity were demonstrated, for Mr Elliott, hesitatingly and even blushingly, it must be admitted, pleaded that he was a "conscientious objector" and wanted the subject remitted to a committee. In this course he was seconded by Mr. Welsh, who very boldly advocated fuller investigation and spoke of children losing their lives through vaccination.

" In Scotland?" ejaculated Dr Ritchie incredulously.
"Yes, in Scotland" persisted Mr Welsh "and I can give the Doctor private information about them if he wishes it".

The "conscientious objectors" found the support of three Councillors, but the overwhelming majority was against interfering with the law.

The Edinburgh Evening News July 1891
Intoxicants in an Edinburgh poorhouse

A meeting held last night in Marshall Street Hall Edinburgh under the presidency of Mister J. Slater. An address was delivered by Mr. Amery of Birmingham Honorary Secretary of the Workhouse Drink Reform League upon drink in pauper institutions. The speaker pointed out that the universal testimony of masters and chaplains of poorhouses and chairmen of Boards of Guardians was that the great bulk of pauperism was due either directly or indirectly to drink, some going so far as to agree with Sir J T D Llewellyn, Chairman of the Swansea Board, that 90 out of every 100 inmates were brought to the workhouse in some way or other through drink. The 463 inmates of the Edinburgh Poorhouse cost the ratepayers for spirits as much as 25,800 paupers elsewhere. After the address a resolution on the motion of Mr. James Hamilton was unanimously agreed to, requesting the Edinburgh parochial authorities consider the advisability of still further reducing or altogether abandoning the use of intoxicants.

The North Briton April 1878
Drinking in Scotch poorhouses

The house Governor of the Abbey Parochial Board Poorhouse in Paisley has prepared a statement showing the consumption of alcoholic liquor per head per annum by sick poor during the last five years in Scotch poorhouses. The lowest consumer is the Poorhouse of East Lothian, where the poor are either all remarkably healthy or semi-teetotallers, the amount expended having been only threepence halfpenny per head per annum. The inmates of the Edinburgh City Poorhouse consumed at the rate of 1s 4½d a head, while those at Saint Cuthbert's required 6s 2½d per head. South Leith Poorhouse is still higher. The sum expended in it being 9s 0¾d per head and even here there must be great abstemious as compared with the expenditure of such poorhouses as Nairn, Sutherland, Skye, Thurso and Peebles. In Thurso Poorhouse the ratio per head is £3 8s 6½d and in Peebles, £3 13s 10½d. The number of sick poor in Edinburgh City Poorhouse is stated at 595, and the consumption being at the rate of 1s 4½d, gives a total of £11 2s 3½d expended annually for alcoholic liquors. There are only five sick poor people in Peebles Workhouse, but they consume £18 0s 6¾d worth of alcoholic liquor per annum.

Glasgow Herald September 1895
Entertainments and Local papers

The minutes of the House Committee bore instruction to the Governors of Craiglockhart and Craig Leith to provide draught boards, swings, skipping ropes and other suitable amusements for adults and children; also, that 18 copies of the evening papers be got for the inmates in Craiglockhart Poorhouse for and 12 copies for Craigleith.

The Scotsman June 1887
Edinburgh City Parochial Board
No walking on our hill

The monthly meeting was held yesterday, the Chairman Mr. W Officer presiding. Mr. Doig moved the disapproval of the minutes relating to the cost to the parish of the omnibus and carriage. He said that the matter had not been properly discussed by the House Committee and he asked the matter be sent back. Mr. MacKenzie said that it had been felt that the expenditure was excessive. The report showed that the subcommittee had had under consideration the disposal of two of the horses at the Poorhouse and as this was still under consideration, the minutes were allowed to pass.

On the motion of Councillor McLaren, the Board unanimously resolved to send a congratulatory address to the Queen in connection with the Jubilee and a small committee was appointed to prepare and transmit the address. The minutes of the House Committee showed that a subcommittee had been appointed on the motion of Mrs. Bow to report whether, in consequence of recent occurrences under the present system, a change was not desirable in the existing medical administration of the Poorhouse. The minutes also showed that the committee had authorized the Governor to give the inmates a treat for the Queen's Jubilee similar to that usually given on New Year's Day.

A letter was read from Mr James Drummond, Secretary of the Craiglockhart-Hydropathic Company, requesting renewal of permission for residents of the Hydropathic to walk on Craiglockhart Hill. Permission was refused on the motion of Mr. Lewis for the reason the permission was formerly "most inconvenient and injurious". The Governor of the Poorhouse asked the sanction of the Board for the lighting of a bonfire and the display of fireworks on West Craiglockhart Hill tonight in celebration of the Jubilee.

Canon Hannan- *"who pays the expenses?"*
Chairman- *"subscription"*
Canon Hannan- *"Oh, that's all right"* (laughter). The sanction was given.

Letter to the Scotsman May 1919
Music for the poor

Sir

Should there be any readers who do not know what a splendid work the members of the Edinburgh Student Christian Unions are doing as regards the conducting of ward services in the Royal Infirmary and Craiglockhart Poorhouse, kindly allow me first to explain briefly what is done before I state my case. A number of students, men and women, visit the Infirmary and the Poorhouse regularly on Sundays, when they conduct short, bright, cheerful services in some of the wards. The greater part of each service is occupied in singing hymns specially selected by the patients and when the services over, each student goes round the ward and has a friendly chat with the patients individually. In this way he tries to impart some cheer and comfort to those whose lives have been stricken with infirmity or disease. The patients themselves had testified freely how much they appreciate the weekly visits of the students. They greatly appreciate the little the students can do for them and are always pleased to see them.

I shall now on straight away deal with the motive for making this appeal, namely the great need there exists for musical instruments (piano or harmoniums) in some of the medical wards in the Poorhouse. Perhaps there is someone who has such an instrument however small it may be, and which is not being used who would be so generous as to present it to us, or who give us the loan of it for the present? May I, on behalf of my fellow students and myself, who conduct these ward services, make this urgent appeal to all sympathetic citizens?

I am etc.
CL Lautre Murray

Yorkshire Evening Post Wednesday November 17th, 1909
Lovemaking in the poorhouse

It Is pleasing to find the romance has not been wholly banished, not even from the poorhouse. Discussion took place at the Edinburgh Parish Council over the erection of a fence at Craiglockhart Poorhouse which had been put there by the Governor because it had been discovered, inter alia, that a nurse or nurses had been in the habit of breaking out at this unguarded point for the purpose of a little surreptitious flirtation.

The Leven Advertiser September 1923
Pauper cost nearly 1000 pounds.

A woman who entered the workhouse 38 years ago with a child and who has just died, cost the ratepayers over £900.

Dropping the title 'Poorhouse'

The Edinburgh Parish Council on Monday agreed on the recommendation of the House Committee to drop the word for 'Poorhouse' from the notice boards at the entrances to Craiglockhart Poorhouse and to substitute the word 'hospital' and amendments to retain the present notices was lost on 27 votes to 13.

Mid Lothian Journal January 1910
Craiglockhart Poorhouse; A New Year's Dinner

The inmates of Craiglockhart Poorhouse were on Thursday last treated as usual to the dinner kindly provided by Mr Oliver Riddell and Mrs Riddell of Craiglockhart House. The rooms and wards had been tastefully decorated and a bright and cheerful appearance was given to the house. Over 800 inmates, including about 100 children, participated in the dinner. Among those present at the dinner were Mr Richard Clark, Chairman of the Parish Council and Mrs Clark, the Reverend John Baird and Mrs Baird, Councillor Stephenson, Captain Morrison, Mr Bennett the Governor and Miss Lawrie the Matron. While the inmates were receiving their dinner in the large hall, the ladies and gentlemen made a tour of the wards and said a kindly word to the occupants. On returning to the hall, Mr Clark took the chair and gave a short address. After wishing them all a Happy New Year, he referred to the kindness and attention bestowed on them by the Governor and the Matron who, he said, did all in their power to promote their comfort and happiness. He then read a letter from Mr and Mrs Riddell who wished them all a Happy New Year and hoped they would enjoy their treat (applause). Mr and Mrs Riddell's kindness was, the Chairman said, exceedingly great and they deserved the gratitude and best wishes of all interested in the institution. (Applause) He concluded by asking three cheers for Mr and Mrs Riddell, a request which was promptly and lustily responded to.

Thereafter the Reverend Mr Baird said a few words to the inmates. At the close the Chairman intimated that he had arranged to have all the children taken to the circus, an announcement which seemed to please the young folks immensely. The dinner which consisted of soup, beef steak pie, plum pudding and as a dessert apples and oranges, seemed to be heartily enjoyed. On finishing the repast, the smokers were presented with a quantity of tobacco and the snuffers with a quantity of snuff.

Scotsman January 1918
Meagre rations

The meeting of Edinburgh Parish Council was held yesterday, Major Huie[14] presiding. The minutes of the House Committee showed that they had had before them a letter from the Local Government Board as to the dietary of the poorhouse inmates, expressing the hope that the consumption of food was according to the scheme of voluntary rationing announced by Sir Arthur Yapp. The Governor of Craiglockhart Poorhouse reported that, having gone very carefully into the matter, the consumption in regard to the items mentioned was actually less than the quantities allowed.

14   Major DH Huie 1863-1938 9th Royal Scots (Territorials). On record guarding German POWs at Redford Barracks in 1914. Commanding Officer Royal Scots Depot E Claremont Street Edinburgh.

Edinburgh Evening News September 1899
Pay and conditions.

The usual monthly meeting of the Edinburgh Parish Council was held today in Castle Terrace. With regard to the terms and conditions of the Chaplain's appointment at Craigleith, it was recommended by the Chairman's Committee that the appointment be for one year and that the Chaplain devote his whole time to the duties of his office and that the Council advertise for candidates, the salary being £150 per annum. Mr Johnston thought this would lead to confusion. It was not definite enough and he would add that the employment be for one year subject to re-election. He moved accordingly. Mr McGibbon moved that the terms be three months' notice on both sides. Mr. Stalker supported Mr. MacKinnon and Mr. Moffat, at some length, contended that the position should be for one year only and not a permanent seat. They wanted a man fresh with the enthusiasm of his high calling, and not one whose ardour was dampened by long experience with the paupers of the Poorhouse. They then would have greater life and greater light brought into the Poorhouse. On the matter being put to the vote, the motion that the employment be for one year subject to re-election received 17 votes, and the amendment was only supported by six members. The clerk was therefore instructed to advertise accordingly.

In moving that Mr. Bennett the Governor of Craiglockhart should be paid an honorarium of £25.00 per annum for so long as the lunatics remain under his charge, Mr. Stalker referred to the extra responsibilities which had recently been placed on Mr. Bennett, and especially the extra burden imposed by the increase of pauper lunatic inmates, owing to the overcrowded state of Morningside Asylum. Mr. Hendry dissented and, in moving an amendment, said that Mr. Bennett was the best paid Governor in Scotland. He found a seconder in Mr. Fraser, who thought the recommendation very peculiar and wished further information. They had, moreover, to consider their other Governor. Mr. Welsh questioned the competency of the proposal. The Chairman explained that it was an honorarium with an addition attached, which made it practically an increase of salary. Mr Johnston said that the increase should be a mere act of justice on the part of the Council. The recommendation was agreed 13 votes to nine.

The following increases of salary were approved Mr. Mowat Assistant Inspector from £100 to £110; Miss Sinclair from £50 to £60.00, the Reverend JHW Johnston Chaplain Craiglockhart £110 to £115 per annum.

No treats

A letter was submitted from the Local Government Board refusing to sanction application of rates upon treats to indoor poor in any shape or form. Both now on previous occasions the Board had given the subject level consideration in all its aspects and considered that such an application of rates would be illegal. Mr. Young expressed himself disappointed and surprised at the nature of the Board's reply, which he considered contrary to the spirit that characterised the present Government in their dealings with the poor. Their request is very moderate, and the cost was to be kept within such limits as the Board approved and the treat confined to the indoor deserving poor. Nothing could have been more reasonable. He moved the matter be held over for a month or two until complete reports from all parts be received.

The Bradford Observer March 1870
The administration of the poor laws in Scotland

The committee of members of the House of Commons met yesterday for the purpose of considering the subject of the working of the poor laws in Scotland. Witnesses were at once called in continuation of the evidence given last session. The Rev. G Rigg of Edinburgh stated that the number of Roman Catholics in Scotland was about 350,000. In Edinburgh Poorhouse there were last year 110 resident paupers and 70 children and many receiving outdoor relief. No one on the Board looked after the Catholic poor and there was no one to take care that the Catholic children should be brought up in the Catholic religion. The witness complained of the practice of bringing up as Protestants the children of Roman Catholic parents and represented that there ought to be one to watch over the interests of the Roman Catholic poor at the Parochial Boards. The practice prevailed of boarding out in Protestant families of Roman Catholic children, in which cases they were frequently proselytised. The rev. gentleman suggested that all Catholic pauper children should be placed under the direction of a Catholic committee, who would take care that they were placed out in families of their own religion, and that none should be placed in Protestant families or kept in workhouses. Half a crown a week was at present the sum allowed for boarding out a child. The orphanage system was far superior to the boarding-house system.

Here was the second Chaplain to have been dismissed in the 1880s.

Edinburgh Evening News December 1899
Dismissing the chaplain

On the recommendation by the House Committee, the council resolved that the Reverend J H W Johnston, Chaplain at Craiglockhart Poorhouse, be asked to tender his resignation. The matter had come before the subcommittee, who arrived at their recommendations on the grounds that the duties attaching to the office had not been satisfactorily discharged. At the meeting of the House Committee, Mr Welch, seconded by Mr McGibbon, moved out the matter be remitted to the subcommittee to meet with Mr Johnston and report, but the amendment was lost by a majority of 10 votes.

Buy locally.

The Council approved a report by the Law Committee to consider and report as to the legality of public companies estimating for the supply of goods to the Parish Council while they have directors members of the Council. Captain Morrison moved that contracts for supplies to the Edinburgh poorhouses should not be entertained from merchants or others not ratepayers in the City of Edinburgh. In speaking to his motion, the Captain said it was not fair or right that a stranger should come from any other part of Scotland to contract, when there were men in the city willing to contract and able to supply goods of equal value. Mr Thompson seconded and considered it only fair that the money should be spent where it was collected. Mr Moffat moved the previous question and stated that it was of grave importance that they should consider the advisability and legality of the matter. He ventured to point out that the motion was highly improper, if not illegal. They were charged with the duty of protecting the interests of the general body of ratepayers and not of any single merchant in the City of Edinburgh. Their business was to buy in the cheapest market and the motion belonged to the thoroughly exploded policy of protection. (Laughter) Mr. Gibson seconded Mr. Moffatt, who was also supported by Mr Campbell Irons, who was of the opinion the motion was illegal and ought to be ruled out of order.

The Musselburgh News April 1909
Craiglockhart Poorhouse Management

At the monthly meeting of the Edinburgh Parish Council on Monday, Mr Gibson the Chairman who presided said that after the full report of the House Committee in regard to Craiglockhart Poorhouse, it appeared to him at least unnecessary for the Council to go into the matter. There were however one or two points upon which he should like to say a word. First, he would like to correct an impression which the press and through them the public had formed, namely that the House Committee at its meeting on the 5th inst. chose to consider the matter in private. That was not so. The House Committee consisted of the whole members of the Council and was a standing committee. The meeting was its ordinary monthly meeting and, like all meetings of standing committees of the Council, was held without reporters being present. The committee however being aware of the anxiety in the public mind to learn what those entrusted with the management of Craiglockhart Poorhouse had to say in reply to certain published criticisms, very properly instructed a report of their proceedings to be published at the earliest opportunity (Applause). Craiglockhart Poorhouse was managed under certain rules and regulations approved by the Local Government Board and if these regulations were not carried out at the Poorhouse, the Local Government Board would soon direct the Council's attention thereto and that being so, it seemed a pity that the Council's critic should have seen fit to drag the name of the Local Government Board into the controversy. The Council were indebted to the Scotsman for causing an independent visit to be made and the results they have published (Applause). The Council had no reason to be dissatisfied therewith and they would welcome and invite visitation and inspection by any ratepayer who felt inclined to do so, at convenient times which the Chairman of the House Committee and Governor would arrange. The House Committee clearly indicated their desire to do all they could to improve the institutions under their care, and he was sure no member of the Council for a moment considered that the institutions under their charge were perfect, and in considering the circumstances, two things had always to be kept in view. First through the unification of the City and St Cuthbert's, the Council had placed under their charge two very large institutions which, with very little addition during the last 13 years, had sufficed to meet the demands the indoor poor and would be sufficient for some time to come; and second, since the appointment of the Royal Commission on the Poor Law and pending the outcome thereof, the Council had felt that it would be inexpedient to enter into any large scheme, and although one could not forecast the nature of the legislation which was likely to follow up on the Commissioners' report, certain reformation in connection with the administration of indoor relief might safely be anticipated. In the meantime, the ratepayers of Edinburgh might rest assured that the regulations laid down for the Council's guidance were being complied with, and that the wants of the sick poor under their charge, notwithstanding the criticism levelled at the Council's administration, were well provided for (Applause). After all that had been said, he thought the best they could do now was to forget the past and look to the future (Applause)

In the course of the discussion which ensued upon the Chairman's statement, Mr Adair entered a protest against what he described as unjust criticism and untrue statements that had been made in the newspapers. He asked the Chairman with regards to Mr Holland's statement, regarding what the President of the Local Government Board had said to him, and which he could not repeat, if the Local Government Board had power to suggest anything with regard to the management of the poorhouses; if there was anything wrong they could they draw attention to it; had they ever done so; and if so, had the Council ever neglected to attend to anything that had emanated from the Local Government Board?

After reading the rules relating to the point, the Chairman said the Board had been quite within their rights. Mr Adair thought if this meant anything, it was an insinuation that the Scottish Local Government Board did not approve of the way these houses were being managed and he protested against that most earnestly. He would like to point out that this gentleman had made a half-hour's visit and that there were 30 ladies and gentlemen who paid regular visits to the houses and spent hours there. Was it possible that they could go with one eye open and one shut or were they blind all together? Of course, they were only human beings and none of them were perfect, but had they not all said in their mind, "what a blessed thing it is that there is such a place such a shelter for these poor people" Mr. Smith said the insinuation was made not only against them, but against the Local Government Board. The only inference to be taken from the conversation referred to, was that there was something wrong which could not be made public. That they should draw the attention of the Local Government Board to the matter. If the Board had anything to say, it was their duty to say it. The insinuation was very ill-pleasing. Mr Hood thought they might have a meeting with Mr Holland, but this suggestion did not meet with the approval of Mr Huie, who complained of the Local Government Board having sent one of their officials with Mr Holland, when that gentleman visited the Poorhouse. It would only have been courteous if they had given notice of the visit. After further discussion it was decided to drop the matter meantime, a motion by Mr Adair to ask the Local Government Board what their position on the matter was and one by Mr Hood to have a meeting with Mr Holland being departed from.

Chapter 5

The inmates

Life in the Poorhouse as an inmate is described here in detail by an anonymous author.

Edinburgh Evening News 5th and 8th September 1905
Life in an Edinburgh poorhouse

The great amount of widespread destitution, which was rampant in Edinburgh last winter and spring, but which was much alleviated by the Lord Provost's Fund, was the cause of filling the poorhouses to overflowing. There is no doubt the substratum of truth in the axiomatic saying as applicable to Scottish character that it bemeans anyone to descend so low in the social scale when it becomes necessary to apply for relief off the rates. Still, many through various unfortunate circumstances will be compelled to resort to this expedient. With your kind permission, the description of life in one of the City Poorhouses, to which I was allocated from Castle Terrace, where the offices of the Edinburgh Parish Council are situate, will perhaps be perused by your readers.

After giving full particulars re name, age, birth-parish, occupation and, most exacting of all, enquiries as to where I had been resident or peregrinated for the previous seven or eight years, I was relegated to Craiglockhart. Of course, I may say en-passant these particulars were substantiated by careful enquiry as, (on being found correct) the parish of settlement was debited with my maintenance so long as I was an inmate. From Castle Terrace to Craiglockhart I was driven in a cab, and on arriving at the gate or receiving house, my letter of identification was taken, and the particulars therefrom were inserted in the poorhouse roll. I was immediately taken charge of by an inmate who acts in the capacity of warder and who saw I had at once the luxury of a bath; after which I was taken to the probationary wards and put to bed. My clothes and anything I had in my possession were carefully annotated and the particulars inscribed on a printed form which was attached to a made-up bundle and which, after being steamed or fumigated, was put into stores to remain until I requested my demission or dismissal. At night and again next morning, I was medically examined by the resident doctor (a lady) and at 10 a.m., after being rigged out in the distinctive clothes of the institution , I was marched, along with the other men who had been admitted the previous day ,to the office in the body of the house where, after getting a number from the clerk, which (the number not the clerk) I afterwards learned coincided with a number of the ward or room in which I was to sleep, I was taken to the day-room and after being there for several minutes, the labour master taught me to go to the " hair house" or oakum[15] room. There was I then in the short space of the day transferred from a liberty loving subject into a pauper! To deal with the subject matter properly, I will take the conduct of the house *scriatim* and under different headings such as work, dietary, classification or rather want of it, hospital treatment, Ins and outs etc. I will treat the various views in as concise a manner to as will not trespass too much on your space.

Work

No doubt there are many persons who pay rates (some unfortunately find it hard to do so) under the impression that to be an inmate of a workhouse there is very little work to be done, save the ordinary routine of attending to the day's regime. To disabuse those minds of such a fallacy, let it be understood that, although the working hours are shorter than those outside, there is little chance of "dodging". The labour master of course is not one of the" milk and water" order and when one considers that he has under his charge considerably over 100 men, his position is no sinecure. The principal industry at Craiglockhart is stick-bunching for firewood and, as it is a

---

15   Picking Oakum was the teasing out of fibres from old ropes by hand. It was very hard on the fingers. It was sold to shipbuilders, who mixed the fibres with tar to caulk and to make matting. It was also one of the commonest forms of hard labour in Victorian prisons.

considerable source of income, I often wondered why it was not more fully developed. The rate of payment from customers is three shillings and eight pence per hundred bunches and to those who retail, 20 extras are given to the 100. There are machines turning out 3000 in bunches daily and the income, at the charge shown from this alone, is computed to be on an average about £25.00 weekly; of course, against that is the original cost of the wood depreciation on stock and proportional share of working expenses.

The other industry, if it can be classified under such, is oakum teasing. As no-one is tasked, the amount done is infinitesimally small for the number of men employed. Of course, I may say that though this work is not so remunerative as stick-bunching, the strong objection against the capable being unemployed has compelled the Committee to devise this other means whereby idleness may be prevented.

Shortly before I left, a new industry was introduced viz. twine looping and wire twisting, either of which forms a part of completed parcel labels. The loops are paid and the rate of half a penny per 1000. Quick manipulators can make 3000 which works out at four and a half pence per diem. As for the wire, the average daily output by one man is about 1000 and for that the handsome sum of tuppence is got by the management. In emphasizing the amounts, I do so because it is rumoured that the firm which supplies and materials pays outside workers more and, if that is the case, then it is the sorry condition of affairs that sweating, not to use a stronger term, should be introduced into a poorhouse. Not that the inmates benefit much more, still it is a point which would bear further elucidation from the ratepayers' point of view.

Painters, joiners, plumbers and shoemakers who are inmates are generally put to their respective trades. Then again, several men are usually employed by the gardener.

I should mention in connection with the firewood delivery in the town that it is undertaken by the inmates themselves and it says very much for their honesty that in only one instance, and that for a trifling amount, was it considered necessary to call in civil interference during the time I was an inmate. I would like to put a point forward in favour of those same stick deliverers i.e. the altogether too distinctive garb in which they parade the town. Of course, there are some case-hardened enough who do not care in what they appear, but against that many a one has not the lost all self-respect, and to be met and recognised by former friends and fellow workmen is very humbling and altogether galling to the hardier Scot, even though, for the time being, he is an inmate of a public institution. My plea is that those who are engaged on this work should be supplied with other than the ordinary workhouse clothes, so as not to make them so prominent a butt of public ridicule, opprobrium or sympathy, as the heart dictates.

The non-diversity of employment or occupation might be further improved if the Brabazon[16] system were introduced. Of course, I may mention that there is a little work done through outside agencies, among some of the classified inmates, both male and female, but all the time I was in there, there were many old men who, if some light and tasteful task had been given them, would certainly not have had the time hang so readily on their hands. I leave this suggestion to the consideration of the House Committee.

Dietary

The dietary may be summarised as plainness, sameness and inadequateness. I have no to "look a gift horse in the mouth", I will be told. I am not speaking for myself individually, but this I can assert, although the scrupulously clean way in which the food is served is admitted, I specifically say, and that without fear of contradiction, that the quantity sanctioned by the Local Government Board is more often under than over the authorized amount. The similarity of the bill of fare soon palls on the most non-epicurean palette, but "needs must when the devil drives" and to the Poorhouse inmate in becomes very nauseating to be dosed with "meal and milk" – "Chief o' Scotia's food" – thrice daily, varied at the dinner hour with broth

---

16 The scheme was initiated in 1882 by Lady Brabazon to provide occupation for non able-bodied inmates of workhouses, with activity such as knitting and embroidery. It was slow to take off until it was realised the products made could be sold and the scheme could be self-financing.

and bread. On Tuesdays and Fridays pea soup or, as it is facetiously, called "Orange Broth" is then substituted for the vegetable broth. Then again what is looked upon as an extra two or three ounces of suet pudding are added to the Wednesday's and Sunday's menu. That applies only to those who had been 10 days continuously in the house. I mention the word "inadequateness" and it is unfortunately too palpably obvious, but only in the quantity allowed, but in the time granted for the taking of the meals, as especially at the dinner hour, the policy of hustle is only too glaringly apparent. To give an example: when the bell rings at 2 o'clock, the dining hall door is opened and seven minutes elapses before the last man is seated. The time taken to the meal is either seven or eight minutes and the hall is cleared again at 2:20 pm, as shown on the clock – altogether too short a time for proper mastication, to say the least. Now a very simple remedy could circumvent all the hurry, and that by causing the bell to ring five minutes before the hour.

There is another matter, when referring to the dinner, which is a cause of much grumbling-among the men especially. I refer to the espionage that goes on continually by the officials in charge, regarding the taking away of some of the bread which the time allowed hinders them from eating. Times without number and in fact it is almost a daily occurrence, the centre officials warn the men of the dire consequences that would follow if they are discovered taking anything out of the hall. Needless to say, that the practice is carried on, but surreptitiously at that. Now I question the legality, if I may use the word, of interference by any one as to what a man does with the allowance, as sanctioned by the Local Government Board.

The Ins and Outs

As the law stands at present time, anyone can claim admission to a poorhouse but only on one condition -and mark the condition- because it carries very considerable weight with what I might describe as the morale of the applicants. When applying there must be some illness, real or assumed, which entitles the person to claim admission. Destitution pure and simple has no differentiating power whereby a one can obtain the Open Sesame. The examination as made by the medical man may be rigidly enough enforced, but I'm afraid that malingering is too often resorted to, and through this means the number of Ins and Outs is continually being added to. At the meeting of the Parish Council authorities of Scotland held in Edinburgh some months ago, this standing source of adding to the actual poor was very minutely discussed, by nothing definite was arrived at. Until an Act is put upon the statute book which will give the local authority stronger prerogatives to deal with this evil, nothing in the shape of a refusal can be entertained. There is, of course, the prejudice which is a strong trait in the character of the Scottish people generally against any one being refused, as through such refusal death might eventuate. Such an extreme view is only conjectural, but it might happen. The status quo ante of the genus is therefore one of the greatest stumbling blocks to poorhouse reform. The remedy, if such could be enforced, lies in complete isolation, curtailment of any privileges such as they are, and the enforcement of tests (subject to the doctor's approval). No doubt this is drastic enough, but if this were the rule, visits of the Ins and Outs would be fewer, and taxation materially reduced.

I had proposed touching several other aspects of poorhouse life, but the exigencies of space must be considered, and with your approval I'll submit my views on the other phases in a further article.

Second Article

Classification

The spirit of camaraderie which exists among the inmates who have for any length of time had been in the house soon gives one an intimate knowledge of the struggles which many have made, before they had been forced to go into the workhouse. Often and more than is generally understood, many are there through stress of circumstances which they could not overcome. The stories of their later struggles to make ends meet would need an abler pen to record. Many who are presently residing in Craiglockhart had been ratepayers for 20 to 30 years and it is very humbling to them to have to mix with the casuals who are "in today and out tomorrow". I have therefore particularised this subject under a special heading. Classification to a very limited extent is given to few, but a wider and more diversified method should be introduced and though no doubt it would mean more thorough investigation as to a person's previous position in life, it would ultimately lead to a better gradation of the inmates and be the means of harmonising to a greater extent the lives of the habitues of the Poorhouse. At present time classification lies in the hands of the Governor. But I, as an examination of those entitled to the benefits which accrue from classified privileges were introduced say by an Enquiry Committee, have no hesitation in saying that it would much ameliorate the lives of those whose only prospect is to spend the rest of their days inside. When on the subject of classification, I should mention there are good number of men and their wives residing in Craiglockhart, and a moot point among them is the very limited time granted for them to foregather. A short half hour from 4 to 4:30 pm on Saturday afternoons is allowed, with this very anomalous proviso, viz. always in the presence of one or more of the officials, who take much interest in any conversation that may be indulged in, no matter how private the confidences are. It is very humiliating.

Hospital

I approach this particular side of poorhouse life with diffidence, for the very simple reason that, although it is a serious statement to make, I do so with this saving clause, that where everyone is supposed to have some malady, there must of necessity to be some but not so bad as others. I am not equivocating however, when I assert that the numbers who had been in hospital from few days to several months, and even years, look upon a residence there as permanent. I am not assuming lack of any medical supervision, but the fact is altogether too true. In my previous article I emphasized what I considered as "malingering" being resorted to by applicants for admission, and the fact remains that there are some who should be out, and men who are in the body of the house who should be in. It would be invidious on my part to particularise specific cases, but I "could a tale unfold". During the time I was in Craiglockhart, it occurred oftener than once, that men and women to were taken to hospital practically in a state of collapse, and rigor mortis would supervene in a few hours. The hospital accommodation to my mind is inadequate, and so long as such a state of matters exists, there can be no alleviation. I am not ascribing any laxity on the part of the doctor or the staff of nurses in hospital. Still, I am forced to the conclusion that in the first place more room is wanted and secondly an understudy is badly needed to help the lady doctor, who has altogether too much work in a community which fluctuates from 650 to 750.

Visiting

The day for visitors to see the inmates is Saturday from noon to 4 pm, and many look upon this time is the only ray of sunshine in their seclusion. Any little perquisites which the visitors bring their friends are often freely divided by the residents and need I say, very much appreciated. Of course, in cases of serious illness, special passes are granted to friends.

Pass days for inmates.

After being continuously an inmate for six clear weeks, any inmate can claim a pass for liberty to go outside for a day. This is usually granted on Saturdays and I am glad to note the fact that it is very seldom abused. Thereafter every four weeks this prerogative is given.

Amusements and reading.

The social side of the inmates is not forgotten. Several times during my residence concerts of a very enjoyable nature were given by outside parties and it goes without saying that they were, if possible, for more heartily enjoyed by the people inside than if they had been paid for. Cinematographic displays were also introduced once or twice and as much thought of. Among the men themselves, the only forms of amusement are one or two sets of dominoes and draughts. Copies of the previous daily and evening newspapers are given each day, and the news read with avidity. Might I make the suggestion in regard to this particular reading of the papers? It is that in the day room where the men gather together after their work is done, a skeleton form should be erected so that the papers might be put up, which would preclude them from going missing as they frequently do.

I had nearly omitted to mention the library, which is under charge of the chaplain, and I am sorry to state that most of the very readable collection of books which are to be got are in a bad and mutilated condition. If greater care was shown by the inmates, I have no doubt that it would materially add to the reading advantages of the library.

In writing these articles, I have striven to give as fair and unbiased a view of poorhouse life as I could, and if I have expressed myself rather forcibly on some points, it has been done with a set idea of trying to procure some slight amelioration in the condition of the inmates as a body, and not from any personal or ulterior object. Speaking personally, any conversation I had with the Governor imbued me with the idea that he was a good example of the saying, *"Suaviter in modo, fortiter in re"* ("Firm in principle, gentle in manner")

Edinburgh Evening News November 1894
Crimean veterans in Edinburgh poorhouses

The meeting of old soldiers was held in Buchanan's Hotel, High Street Edinburgh last night to consider the case of John MacPherson, the Crimean veteran, late of the Scots Greys and recently an inmate in Saint Cuthbert's Poorhouse. Over 30 were present including several Crimean comrades of MacPherson. The Chairman Mr. Ritchie, Scots Greys, read letters from sympathisers and after some conversation, a committee of 13 "Old Greys" with Mr. Ritchie, Chairman, was appointed to consider suggestions as to the relief of McPherson, and report to a meeting to be held on Tuesday next. Mr. James Dick who had been invited to be present stated in reply to enquiries that MacPherson had been removed from the Poorhouse by two doctors and was presently being provided for by them. It was resolved on the motion of Mr. James Ritchie, late 79th Highlanders and seconded by Mr. Wright late 91st Highlanders, that the public had been made aware through Mr Kinnaird that it was an entire fallacy to suppose that all Crimean veterans had been provided for and action be consistently taken to that end. A letter was read calling attention to the case of Felix MacDonald who had served in the 6th Dragoons and had been for nearly eight years an inmate of Craiglockhart Poorhouse. He had gone through the Crimean War and the Indian Mutiny and had received medals for Balaclava, Sebastopol and Lucknow. Mr. Ritchie also drew attention to the case of Sergeant Bremner, late the 79th Highlanders, now an inmate of Leith Poorhouse. Bremner was a victim to rheumatics as a result of the first winter in the Crimea. A year ago, he made an application for relief from the veterans' fund, but he was informed he had no claim, as he had purchased his discharge. Mr Richie said it was their duty to give publicity to such a scandal. The fund is got up solely for men who had gone through the Crimea and Indian Mutiny, irrespective of length of service. The committee should be formed for the purpose of bringing public opinion to bear in some way. Mr. Ewing late 42nd Highlanders said a public meeting should be convened and they should ask the Lord Provost to preside and many gentlemen of military experience or whose sympathies were with them would no doubt assist. A great mistake was made in sending money to England. They should keep their money in Scotland for so they could distribute it as a thought proper.

The Evening Telegraph November 1894
Crimean veteran in an Edinburgh poorhouse

John MacPherson, 70 years of age, a Crimean veteran lies at present in the hospital at the Poorhouse in Edinburgh. In early in life, he enlisted in the Scots Greys, served in the army for 13 years, went through the Crimean war and received his discharge at its close. He took part in the famous charge at Balaclava, where he was slightly wounded, and he has a British Crimean war medal and the Turkish medal. At one time he was a book canvasser, but for a number of years until recently worked in the laboratory of one of the medical professors at Edinburgh University. His wife and three children died years ago and having no known relatives, the lonely old man after many ups and downs at length finds himself, with health broken by a paralytic shock, a charge upon the parochial authorities. An effort is to be made to bring his case before the Commissioners of Chelsea Hospital who have the distribution of the fund for Crimean and Indian veterans.

The Edinburgh Evening News October 1884
Death of an Edinburgh centenarian

There has just died in the City Poorhouse Edinburgh, an old man named John Munro, who is reputed to have attained the age of 103 years and six months. Munro was born at Logie in Ross-shire and during the disastrous campaign against the Americans in 1812 to 15, he served in the British Army. He was for 10 years a letter-carrier in the General Post Office Edinburgh and afterwards a Butler. With his wife he was admitted into the poorhouse four years ago and the latter died in 1882 at the age of 83. Before admission to the poorhouse, the aged couple had earned a maintenance by keeping a mangle, but with advancing years their health gave way, and they were obliged to request parochial assistance.

The Evening Telegraph August 1877
A centenarian in Craiglockhart Poorhouse

Interesting reminiscences from this morning's Edinburgh Courant

Through the courtesy of Doctor Furley, the medical officer of Craiglockhart Poorhouse, I was introduced the other day to an inmate, who declares that he was born in 1776 and that he is consequently 101 years of age. His name is John Cameron MacLeod, and his occupation has been that of a tailor. He says he was born on the coast of Australia, his father being a seaman and that he is of Highland extraction. To appearance he is not more than 75 years of age; his intellect is clear – the sharpest indeed in the ward, according to the testimony of the attendants; his eye is undimmed, having received "the second sight", his hearing is unimpaired, his skin is almost without a wrinkle, the only apparent defect being that he has to walk on crutches, owing to his thigh for having been lately broken by a fall. The fracture has united in a wonderfully short space of time and he looks forward to being soon set at liberty to wander about the country, as he has done for several years, without any fixed place of abode. That he is a most intelligent man there can be no doubt, and the minuteness with which he describes events which took place in his early days is very remarkable. One would be apt to suppose that his descriptions of persons with whom he has come into contact and the scenes which he has witnessed are purely imaginary comments, were it not that during the three or four months he has resided in the poorhouse, he has never shown the slightest aberration of mind or tendency to hallucinations. Without of course being prepared to accept without further evidence the accuracy of the old man's statements, I will give an outline of the conversation I had with him in a poorhouse.

You certainly do not appear to be more than 75 years of age?
Well sir, I was a grown-up man 75 years ago, for I was born in 1776.

Are there any circumstances which lead you to fix on 1776 as your date of birth?
There are various circumstances; but I may mention one of which there can be no doubt whatever, that I joined the Essex Volunteers in 1794, when I was in my 18th year. At that time there was a dread of rebellion in Ireland.

Do you recollect the names of any of the officers in your corps?
I well remember Adjutant Stubbs and there was a Captain Frenery, who called himself Fleney. His wife was a proud headed woman and wished to change the name.

What did your uniform consist of?
It was a blue dress with two rows of buttons down the front, besides the row that fastened the coat. The coat was round, like the slop-jackets now worn by the soldiers. For arms we had the old firelocks of course, with bayonets to match. The cap was made of some kind of hair manufactured into a light cloth and it had a small peak. It had upon it the letters "RV" for Royal Volunteers and on the firelocks "Geo. III "was engraved.

Do you remember any other incidents of your early life?
I remember seeing Nelson with his one hand. I also remember seeing Burns the poet. I will tell you about him afterwards. I saw Tom Paine – the wretched Paine. That was about 1791. I also remember seeing and speaking to John Wesley, the great preacher. One day he asked me if I was to be a Methodist. I said no, I would rather be a Clarkeite, if I were

to be anything. The Clarkeites, you may know, where the followers of Dr. Adam Clarke the celebrated commentator[17]. I was a young lad when I saw Burns. A Miss Clark came to a shop where I was and was talking about the making of a riding-hood or riding-dress, when she pointed out Burns, who was there at the time. I do not recollect all he said, but that I remember he gave me an advice to save what I could in early life. In the words of his song:

"Not for to hide it in a hedge
Nor for a train attendant:
But for the glorious privilege
Of being independent"

With whom did you learn to be a tailor?

When my father and mother came home from the sea, they went to Inverness. My father's name is John MacLeod and my mother's Janet Cameron. My mother died when I was about nine years of age. I left the house because I found that my father was to marry again. I had a strong desire to join my brothers, who were in the army. Two of them were in the 42nd Highlanders[18] and three in the 92nd [19] or "Yellow Hielanders" as they were called. They all fell at Waterloo. By getting my coach fare paid part of the way, I reached my brothers in the 92nd who were at a place near Gosport. I could not pass for a soldier myself as one of my toes was somewhat deformed and is so still. I became an apprentice however with the master tailor in the 92nd regiment and wherever they went in Britain I went with them. I had been nearly four years with them when the Master Tailor died, and I had three years of my apprenticeship to run. I ultimately went to Mr. Cox an army tailor and contractor at Canterbury; and also, I worked there with a Mr. Leslie. After both these gentlemen died, I came across the border and worked with the person in the name of Lamb near Hawick. I was 47 years in England altogether and I came to Glasgow in the year 1838 and left it in 1846. I was with the firm of Keevan and Bootle, who has a place at the corner of Saint Enoch's lane, afterwards Allan and Stewart's.

---

17   Adam Clarke Methodist theologian and biblical scholar 1762-1832
18   42nd Regiment of Foot aka The Black Watch
19   92nd (Gordon Highlanders) Regiment of Foot, raised in 1794.

Are there any other circumstances which lead you to fix your age at 101?
Yes, when I was about 50 years of age, I was employed by Mr. Cox to go with the 'Kent', an East Indiaman bound for Bengal and China with quantity of clothes for the troops in the East. The clothes were not made up but had to be fitted on after being sent abroad as there were great differences in the size of the men. The ship went on fire, as you know, and it was soon seen that there was no hope for it. The deck soon became so hot that we could hardly stand upon it. I recollect when a voice called out there was a sail in sight that there was not a dry eye on board. The sail proved to be that of the brig 'Cambria'[20] commanded by Captain Cobb. There were nearly 800 persons on board the Kent and so thronged was the Cambria after we went or board that a candle would scarcely burn below. Four sailors who had stepped on the magazine of the Kent were blown up. There was a Mr. Upton, a private passenger on board who belonged to Hawick, I think. I was in communication with him some time afterwards. The loss of the Kent occurred in the year 1825. There were 82 lives lost. I scrawled the first narrative of the wreck. I think it went to the Tract Society, Paternoster Row, for publication. While speaking of this, I may state that I wrote a little book called "The Tailor's Cutting Room".

Did you go abroad with a 92nd Highlanders?
No, but I always took great interest in the regiment, as my brothers were in it. The two who were in the 42nd changed to the 92[nd, so] that they might be together. They had some difficulty in getting together, as it was thought five of one family were too many in one regiment. Before the battle of Waterloo, I got leave by special charter from the Prince Regent to visit my brothers, which I did. I do not think that Buckingham Palace was in existence at that time. It was after considerable difficulty that I got admission to the Prince Regent at the Tower, where I presented my application and where I saw his father, George III. The King appeared to be a good fellow, but he spoke in broken German. And the Prince seemed to be a good businessman. On leaving, I got some money from the Prince.

---

20 In 1825 the East Indiaman 'Kent' with 600 aboard caught fire in a gale off Spain. The lantern of a sailor inspecting damage ignited a cask of spirits. Miraculously, the small brig Cambria saw the burning ship and fought through towering seas to rescue nearly all the men women and children aboard. The event was commemorated by the poet McGonagall in his inimitable way (Appendix 1)

SAVED FROM THE WRECK.

Are there any persons to whom you could refer to as having known you?
There is a Dr Whittaker in Glasgow, who knows me. I was well acquainted with the late Dr. Norman MacLeod, was a great friend to me.

Do you belong to the same MacLeods?
I never claimed kindred with him, and I do not say the that I am of the same MacLeods. All I say is that he was a very kind friend to me. And MacLeods to whom I belong are a long-lived family. My grandfather drew military pay for 91 years.

In answer to other questions, he said that he was at one time in possession of a black-letter Bible[21], in which he had written details regarding his life and family. He had lent it to some person in the south of Scotland who had never returned it. His sight having failed him, he used spectacles when he was between 50 and 80 years of age, but since his sight returned, he had been able to read the smallest print. He never smoked or took snuff and was always sparing in the use of spirits. He was a bachelor and had not been in the habit of "cheeking up" to the ladies. In closing the conversation, which but for want of time on my part might have been carried on for hours, so chatty was the old man, he expressed himself deeply grateful for the attention paid to him in the poorhouse and especially to Dr. Furley and the resident surgeon for the care bestowed on his broken limb.

Dundee Courier and Advertiser 4th December 1929
Dead woman "alive"
Case of mistaken identity
Dundee native traced on the eve of her funeral

Unusual circumstances have attended the identification of a woman who was found drowned in the River Esk Midlothian. The body was discovered towards the end of last week in the water near the Victoria Bridge Musselburgh and soon afterwards was identified is that of Mary Haggerstone aged 55, a native of Dundee.

---

21   Gothic script typeface

The Inmates

She had applied to the Inspector of Poor at Musselburgh some time earlier for relief for and had been directed to the Inveresk Poorhouse, where she remained for a couple of days. She then disappeared along with another woman. The body was identified by the Musselburgh poor relief officer and afterwards a relative of Haggerstone came through from Edinburgh and confirmed the identification. Arrangements were made that she would be buried on Monday afternoon.

Police inquiries

Meanwhile however the police made enquiries regarding the whereabouts of the second woman who might be able to give some information as to how the dead woman met her end. At the Craiglockhart Poorhouse Edinburgh they found, to their surprise, not only the woman they were looking for, but also the Dundee woman. If she had not been found in time, she would have been officially posted as buried.

Yesterday morning the body was identified by relatives is that of Mrs. Helen Tully 61, of Oakbank, a widow who resided alone and whom had been missing from home since the middle of last week.

Edinburgh Evening News July 1893
Edinburgh Parish Council

A difference appears to have taken place between Mr. Councillor Younger and the Governor of Craiglockhart Poorhouse. The councillor considered that an apology was due to him. The matter came before the House Committee on 1st June. From the correspondence reading it appeared that Mr. Councillor Younger alleged the Governor behaved to him in a rude manner. A letter was written by the Governor, in which he expressed regret that if, in the irritation of the moment, he had used an expression which might be constructed as discourteous, but that was not considered ample by the Councillor. After discussion the motion was unanimously passed let the matter drop and to take no further action.

A motion stood on the billet today in Mr. Williamson's name for desiring it to be remitted to the Finance Committee to inquire into the different methods and respect of costs to be adopted for borrowing money from respective banks. Mr. Williamson said he was pleased to see that the Finance Committee had come to be of his opinion, which he had been laying before them for a twelvemonth. (Laughter). That committee had already taken steps to get the information he desired and therefore his motion would drop. Mr. Dallas retorted that the Finance Committee had only done its duty.

Mr. Heron had given notice of motion requiring them all persons male or female who were admitted to the Poorhouse three times within six months should be put to the test sheds, compelled to work on Saturday afternoons, have their meals separately from the other inmates and be generally isolated. He spoke of the trouble which these occasional visitors cost. While they stated they had rheumatism and other complaints, it was frequently the case that laziness was their sole ailment. Miss Phoebe Blyth said it was desirable to put a stop to these people going out and in, if at all possible, but she objected to all those punishments being imposed at once. After some discussion Mr. Heron withdrew his motion in favour of one proposed by Mr. Irons, that the matter should be remitted to a committee to consider and report as to dealing with the class who most frequently visited the Poorhouse. This was the most important question of the day he considered for which they, as poor law guardians, had had to deal with. He thought they should consider the matter thoroughly and get advice if necessary. That was all the business of importance.

Ladies and gentlemen interested in golf were asked to remain behind for a little.

Aberdeen Press and Journal September 1927
Foundling

Wrapped in a piece of blanket and two pieces of a cotton sheet the newly born a male child was found lying on the grass at the side of the road leading to the Poorhouse off Colinton. The child is stated to be strong and healthy. It was taken to Craiglockhart Poorhouse hospital to which is being cared for. Meanwhile investigations are being made by the police to trace the mother of the child.

Edinburgh Evening News September 1893
The pauper in a cab shelter

An inmate of Craiglockhart Poorhouse named Mary Finnegan pleaded guilty to having yesterday been found lying in the cab shelter at Haymarket Terrace with a child three years of age under her charge. The accused stated she left Craiglockhart Poorhouse to visit her father. It appears she was unable to find her father and she intended spending the night in the shelter and to go back to the Poorhouse next day. The Sheriff remitted her back to the Poorhouse authorities.

Edinburgh Evening News September 1897
Scene in an Edinburgh church

May McCormack, a young poorly clad woman carrying a child, was brought to the bar of Edinburgh City Police Court today, Sheriff Substitute Sym on the bench, charged with having on Thursday last created a breach of the peace in Saint Patrick's Roman Catholic Chapel. Evidence was led. Charles Gallacher stated that he was passing the chapel when he saw a small crowd collected at the door. On going he found the accused yelling and very much excited, a crowd of children gathered round her. He also saw her rushing about the church and going up to the altar. Witness then went for a constable who arrested the accused. Catherine Judge stated that she saw the accused conducting herself in a very outrageous manner in the chapel. The accused afterwards rushed up to the baptismal font in the centre of the chapel and dipped her child in holy water. The clergy and two constables ultimately arrived on the scene. The accused said to the Sheriff she had been an inmate of Craiglockhart Poorhouse and that she was willing to go back again. Sheriff said he thought the accused the poor weak creature and that she would be better in the Poorhouse. Although she was quite sane, he thought she would be the better of being kept until the Poorhouse authorities send for her. The accused was thereafter removed to the cells.

Edinburgh Evening News October 1897
Violins for lunatic paupers

The following excerpts from the medical committee minutes of Edinburgh Parish Council shows what is done by them to promote the welfare of boarded out lunacy patients. James Hamilton this patient takes delight in playing the violin and has been using one belonging to the Guardian's son, but he has now left the district. Remitted to the inspector to provide him with a second hand one.

The Edinburgh Parish Council remitted to Messrs. Stalker and Dunlop to confer with the Governor of Craiglockhart Poorhouse to obtain an estimate regarding the laying out of a bowling green there for the amusement of the lunatic patients. The Chairman's committee, it appeared, had unanimously agreed to recommend the council that it was inadvisable to fit up electric light in the poorhouses and in the Chambers at Castle Terrace. Mr. Arnot moved that this matter should be remitted to the committee to ascertain exactly what the cost of the change would be. This was agreed to by 12 votes to four. There seemed to be a desire that the Chambers at least should be lit by electricity.

Mid Lothian Journal March 1902
Saved up

Recently there died in Craiglockhart Poorhouse a lunatic pauper, upon whom the City Parish had expended since he became chargeable in 1888, the sum of £377 14s 10d. At his death. a bank book with the Savings Bank, showing a balance of £17 15s 2d. was found in his possession, but how he received or accumulated the money was not known. He had evidently, in spite of his mental derangement, been 'cute enough' in some things, for Mr Ferrier, the Clerk, informed the Council on Monday that he had described himself in taking out the book as "Assistant, Craiglockhart Poorhouse". When the laughter which greeted this announcement had subsided, the Clerk ventured the opinion that some charitable person had been in the habit of giving him money, as he, having been employed as a messenger, had been honest and trustworthy.

Chapter 6
Medical Care

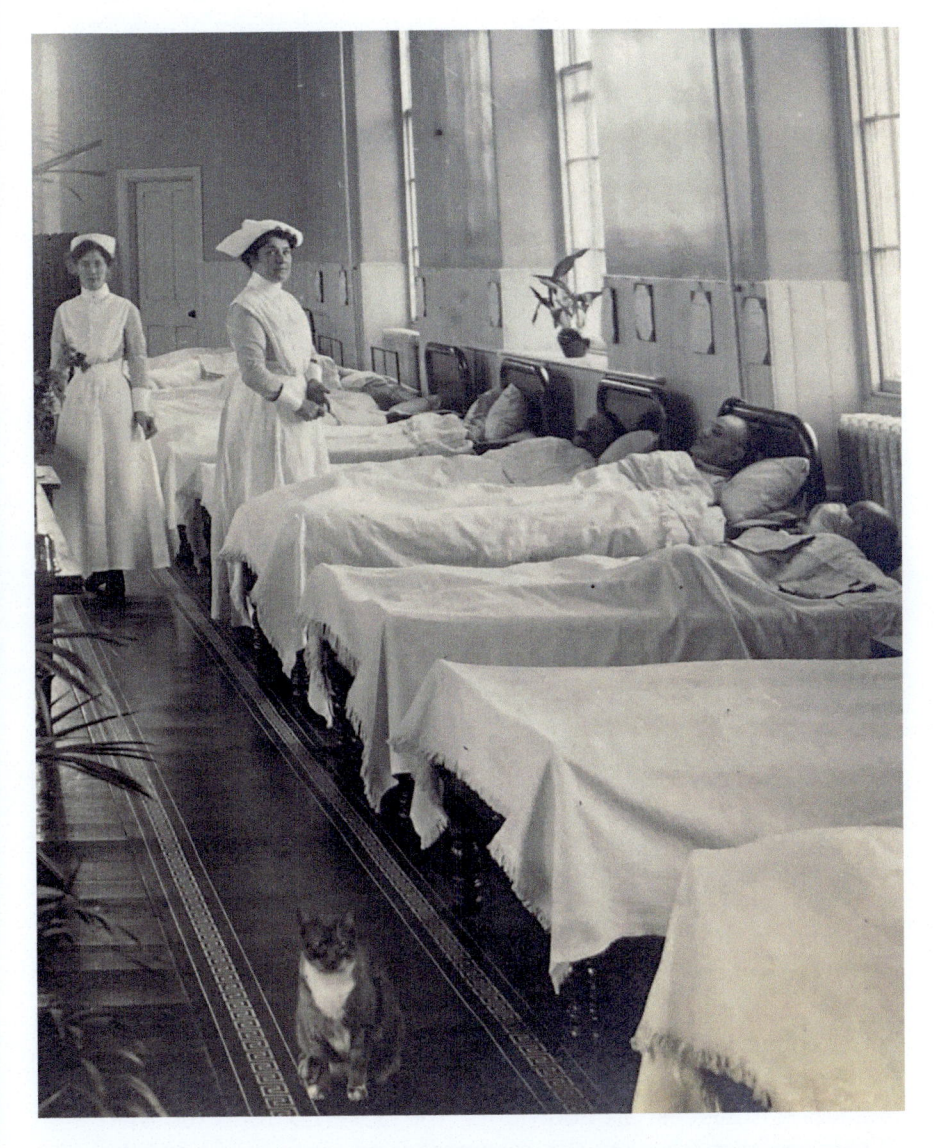

The presence of the cat in the ward presumably kept the mice down.

The Scotsman March 1906
Inadequate poorhouse accommodation

The minutes of the House Committee dated fifth of March bore that a letter had been received from the Local Government Board asking the Committee to consider as to the advisability of erecting at Craiglockhart Poorhouse an observation block for mental cases and to consider as to fitting up an operating room in the hospitals of both poorhouses for in accordance with the requirements of the institutions.

The report of the house governor of Craiglockhart Poorhouse stated that, though the accommodation in the main house had frequently been taxed to the limit, there had been no overcrowding in any of the wards. The staff of servants was quite adequate, and the dietary was carried out according to regulations laid down by the Local Government Board. The medical officers report stated that the accommodation as a whole was too limited, but relief from overcrowding was gained by working in conjunction with Craiglockhart. When the two poorhouses were considered together, he believed that the accommodation as a whole was still far below the needs of the Parish. As regarded the accommodation for classes, he believed the main house so far as it went was fairly good. In the hospital for there was greater need for smaller rooms on wards so as to get better classification of obnoxious, noisy or isolation cases. With regards to the accommodation, he urged the division of one of the wards into small rooms. Failing that, the establishment somewhere of a small room for conducting operations seemed to him most necessary. The General Health of the inmates seems to be as good as their circumstances and their age permitted. It was worth mentioning that in reviewing the death rate for the last six months, he had found the mortality had been reduced to exactly half what he had been accustomed to estimate as the average. He did not know the cause but probably was due to a temporary accumulation of aged persons in the house.

Regarding Craiglockhart Poorhouse, the Governor reported that during the past winter to the accommodation was found by totally

Medical Care

inadequate. The daily average number of children in the Poorhouse for the year was 116. The medical officer suggested the erection of a block intermediate between house and hospital for those cases of phthisis[22] which were not sufficiently ill for hospital but not exactly suited for the main house. Consideration of the question of insufficiency of accommodation has been delayed meantime. A letter was read from the City of Edinburgh Charity Organization asking the Council to appoint five of their members to act on the council of the society. There was a recommendation from the House Committee that the distress committee be approached to supply men to form a road round Craiglockhart Hill and a boundary wall between the Poorhouse and the City Hospital, the Council merely to supply the material and implements and a committee to supply the men and pay them. After discussion power was given to proceed with the making of the road if the distress committee agreed to supply the labour. The question of the erection of the wall was remitted to the House Committee with powers to confer with the Town Council and the Distress Committee and to proceed with the work if thought fit.

---

22   Pulmonary tuberculosis

The Mid Lothian Journal January 1908
The overcrowding of the Poorhouse Hospitals

The Parish Council discussion was opened by Mr. Gibson, who proposed that the Council adopt the principle of providing additional accommodation at Craiglockhart to relieve the congestion in the poorhouse hospitals. It would he said be simply ridiculous for them at that point and to go and take land at Craigleith at probably £50.00 per acre. They could not do better than go on the lines of having iron and wood buildings for hospitals. They found not only in the West of Scotland, but also in England, that instead of putting up permanent buildings for such purposes, they were erecting moveable or iron buildings. These were being readily put forward by county councils and other boards for the use of hospitals. Mr. Johnston suggested that they erected buildings on the Woodilee System[23] for a children's hospital. Councillor Walsh seconded,

Mr. Bennett, the Governor of Craiglockhart, replying to a question, mentioned that there were present in Craiglockhart 25 phthisical patients. 18 of these are in one ward and the others are placed in other parts of the hospital. They had no alternative but to put these patients among other cases. Father Stewart moved an amendment that they do not put up any new buildings in the meantime at either Craiglockhart or at Craigleith but meet this question of overcrowding in the hospitals by sending some of their paupers to other poorhouses throughout the country, which it was said were almost half empty. He did not wish to see any buildings put up in the meantime, because he expected something very great from the "test class" question which had just been settled. Then again, they would soon have the use of the Governor's house in Craigleith as hospital accommodation. A number of the members of the Council seem to have got the Woodilee system of building on the brain. He thought it would probably be a great success, but he would like to see it tried first at Bangour. Mr. Ferrier suggested that Father Stewart

---

23   Woodilee Lunatic Pauper Asylum in Lenzie. Adopted a pioneering system of unlocked doors, and rather than prison-like wards and restraints, patients were given activities, ranging from crafts to site maintenance. Patients were free to roam the grounds, rather than be confined to "airing courts".

should alter his amendment so that it might read that enquiries should be made regarding the sending of paupers to the poorhouses and Father Stuart agreed to that. Mr. Williamson asked the clerk if they had paupers in their houses who belonged to other parishes. Mr. Ferrier replied that they had over 60 when the last information on that point was received. They were always coming and going, but they had already taken steps to get quit of them. Councillor Currie suggested they should keep the phthisical patients apart and he moved that they consider the question of erecting a separate pavilion for them. Mr. Nichol moved that a small committee be appointed to bring in a report on the whole subject. Dr. McRae said it would be a wise thing if they could do something to place the phthisical patients in a separate hospital from other patients. For a beginning, it would be quite sufficient to erect an iron building for 30 or 40 of these patients.

Mr Farquharson seconded the amendment. Mr Kerr said that in all his six years' experience, the hospital question had always been a crying evil. They had always been a mess with their hospitals. He thought it very necessary besides building a pavilion for phthisical patients, that they should have a hospital building at Craiglockhart. If they had such a building, Craigleith could also be relieved. Mr. Anderson doubted if there was an absolute necessity for these buildings and he questioned if they were justified in going to this expenditure. He held that it was not the duty of the Parish Council to put up separate hospital accommodation for phthisical patients. Father Stewart then agreed to withdraw his amendment in favour of a proposal by Mr. Nichol. The Chairman said it was quite clear that their hospitals and houses were so much congested that they must take steps to provide a remedy. They had been at this stage for years and it seemed to him that this was just another case of Bangour hanging up the matter for a period. With regards to the question of sick rooms, he asked how they were to get sick rooms without building them? They had not accommodation at the present time. The Chairman said that these wood and iron buildings could be erected in six weeks' time. Far too much he said was being made of the extra accommodation which they would have when the Governor of Craigleith went into his new house. On a vote Mr. Gibson's motion was carried by 13 votes to nine after further discussion it was agreed to appoint a committee to select a site in Craiglockhart and to report on what was absolutely necessary.

Edinburgh Parish Council and consumption

A report by a subcommittee of the Parish Council as to checking and curing consumption was submitted to the meeting. In considering the subject, it has to be born in view at the outset that the number of phthisical patients in Edinburgh, according to Sir Henry Littlejohn's report, cannot be less than 5000 while the death rate per 1000 in 1887 was that of a total 19 and in 1897 the total of 18 from phthisis. Though these figures, if really reliable, are highly satisfactory and show a diminishing death rate during this decade, no doubt due to improved sanitation, better house accommodation and increased comfort and living generally, they yet establish the fact that phthisis bears an undesirable proportion of the total death rate. That the subject ought to be one of great interest to the Parish Council is established by the fact that no less than 38.9 of the deaths took place amongst those who lived in houses under £10 rental. The deaths in the Poorhouse at Craigleith were in 1896-97-98, 26,31 and 28 from tuberculosis, almost all pulmonary consumption. In Craiglockhart, the net mortality is about 40 per cent from phthisis, leaving about 60 per

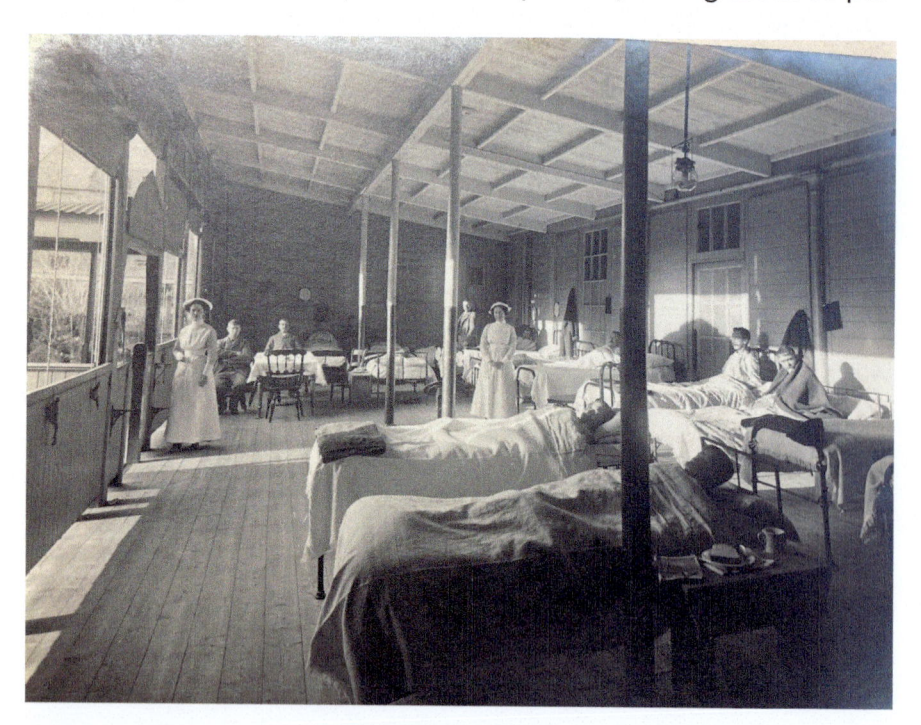

Medical Care

cent benefited by treatment. Now, in the first place it is accepted by all competent authorities that from the experiments made in Germany, France, Switzerland and America and England, tuberculosis, or what is popularly known as consumption, can not only be checked by proper measures, but cured in its earlier stages, while it is at the same time admitted that the disease is the one most easily disseminated amongst the population, and causes the largest ravages amongst the community. It does become a duty on all public authorities, and especially Parish Councils to do what they can to minimize the effects of this dire malady and to stimulate and educate the people to protect themselves against its inroads.

The most pressing question as a Parish Council is what should be done with regard to the consumptive patients in the respective poorhouses? All are agreed that the separation of phthisical or consumptive cases from ordinary hospital cases is not only desirable but an absolute necessity. To do this will necessitate additional building in any case. Your Committee therefore consider that it would be advantageous to erect separate consumptive wards at one or other of the houses. The question is, at which? The doctor at each house naturally thinks that the site of the house he has charge of would be best and it is therefore for the Councill to decide. Your Committee consider that the site to the west of Craiglockhart House is probably the most suitable, it has many advantages. It faces the South, is sheltered from the North and east winds, the soil is dry and there are ample facilities for gradual hill climbing. The situation is very favourable, being away from traffic, free from dust, and with a climate not unlike Nordrach[24], where highly favourable results have been obtained. With regards to outdoor cases it is feared that at present not much more can be done and to get visiting doctors, inspectors and nurses to impress on the patients the necessity of not allowing the expectorations to fall upon the floor, but to have spittoons provided, containing some disinfectant such as a solution of carbolic acid, which should be frequently cleaned,- the spitting in handkerchiefs should be avoided and if pieces of rag or paper be used, that they should be burned and not left lying about. That the bedding of consumptives be disinfected and in cases of

---

24 The Nordrach Clinic in Baden Wurttemberg, Germany, founded for the treatment of tuberculosis.

death, the room also should be disinfected. An abundance of light and air should be admitted to all parts by open windows and doors, and strict cleanliness be enforced. Where there are young children, the milk should be boiled overnight. A printed leaflet to this or similar affect pasted on board might be circulated and asked to be hung up in all the houses of pauper consumptives for guidance.

Edinburgh Evening News February 1874
At the Edinburgh Parochial Board

The inspector reported that the various classes of poor chargeable to the parish were as follows adults 476 Males and 981 females, children 229 Males and 323 females. Of these however there were claims made against other parishes for 81 adults and 37 children. The House Committee recommended that itch and venereal wards should be erected at the Craiglockhart Poorhouse in terms of a report and plans by Messrs. Beattie and Sons architects. A discussion took place on the propriety of going to further expense of providing such accommodations and ultimately the subject was referred back to the House Committee to report more fully on the matter between them.

The Scotsman 6th April 1909

In 1909 the Minority Report was one of two reports published by the Royal Commission on the Poor Laws and Relief of Distress 1905-1909, led by Beatrice Webb (of Sydney and Beatrice Webb fame, founders of the Fabian Society and the London School of Economics). The report was ultimately largely disregarded by the Liberal Government of the time but proved a strong influence on the Beveridge reforms 35 years later. The report argued that an individualised approach did not take account of the structural causes of poverty and proposed the break-up of the existing system of poor relief, to be replaced by state provision. Evidently, references to research in Scotland by the Commission and a subsequent letter to the Scotsman clearly caused indignation at the Edinburgh Parish Council. The reader may conclude the Chairman's summing up seems to somewhat undermine the protestations!

The allegations against Craiglockhart Poorhouse

A meeting of the House Committee of Edinburgh Parish Council was held yesterday afternoon at which statements were read with reference to the allegations made by Mr. Sydney Holland, Chairman of the London Hospital, in a letter to the Scotsman regarding Craiglockhart Poorhouse. The meeting was conducted in private and at the close a report was communicated.

Mr. Brydon Hogg, Vice Chairman who presided, first referred to the following passage regarding – "one of the most important poorhouses in Scotland" in the Minority Report of the Poor Law Commission:" in one of the workhouses there were about 600, in the other about 800 inmates of all kinds, the numbers rising 25 to 30 per cent in the winter. For each of these vast workhouses has only a single resident medical officer, in both cases a young woman. Aided only by consultant visiting thrice a week, her duties were to examine thoroughly every inmate on entrance, in order to discover what exactly was his or her disease or infirmity; to certify which of the adults – all presumably non able-bodied, were fit for the test (work); to settle the diet and treatment of all persons actually sick; and to supervise the arrangements for the children and infants.

In each of the workhouses the hospital cases alone numbered between two and three hundred. In one of them at any rate there was a phthisical ward, a surgical ward, an ophthalmic ward, a lying-in ward and, strangely enough, male venereal wards, all under the sole charge of the same young lady doctor who had the medical supervision of the rest of the establishment. The nursing staff was far below an English standard, extensive use being made of pauper inmates. In many of the large wards that I entered, there was no trained nurse in attendance, even in the daytime. In one of these institutions (I forgot to ask in the other) there were only three night nurses for all the hundreds of patients. The operations – some abdominal sections and others of apparent difficulty were performed by the same young lady doctor with the help of the consultant who was a physician! No record of the results was kept. The same young lady doctor had to extract the teeth of the patients requiring this service. Altogether I venture to suggest to the Commission that the condition of the hospital wards in these two large workhouses demands special investigation".

A deplorable circumstance

Those who had time and opportunity to read the report of the Poor Law Commission, the Chairman added, were aware of the paragraph in the Minority Report, but as no poorhouse was specially named, the Edinburgh Parish Council were not called upon to deal with it. However, they gathered from Mr. Sydney Holland's letter in the *Scotsman*, based upon information supplied to him by Mrs. Sydney Webb, the one of the Commissioners that the paragraph referred specially to the poorhouses of Edinburgh. The allegations or animadversions made by him were, in the main, a repetition of the statement in the paragraph of the Minority Report, which statement, he said, after what appeared to have been a hurried visit to Scotland, he found all true. While admitting that the Minority Report contained much valuable information and gave many commendable recommendations, it seemed to the Chairman most deplorable to find that, in spite of repeated public protests by members of the majority and especially by the chairman of the Commission, members of the minority than continue to furnish special information to interested parties before such information was given to the public, and it was still further to be deplored that any honourable gentleman holding a high position in civil life, should, acting on such information, privately visit an institution, without in any way communicating with those responsible for its administration publicly charge their officials with incompetency and the Parish Council with neglect of duty. Such a course of conduct was not only discourteous but, in the Chairman's opinion, not calculated to enhance either the dignity or amenity of public life. At the date of the Visiting Committee's visit, the number of inmates in Craigleith Poorhouse was 598 and the highest during the past winter was 710. In Craiglockhart at the date of the visit, the number of inmates was 702, the highest number during the winter having been 886. As regards the numbers in the poorhouses at the date of the committee's visit and the percentage of increases in the winter months, it would be seen that the statement of the Visiting Committee is, to say the least of it, incorrect. The Visiting Committee said that each of the workhouses had only a single

Medical Care

resident medical officer-in both cases a young woman. The statement was quite correct. The lady doctors now in the service of the Parish Council were duly qualified for the offices they filled. They held degrees of Scottish Universities equal to the degrees issued by the medical schools and Universities of England. Moreover, both these lady doctors had considerable experience of the work of such an institution prior to their obtaining their present appointments. The lady resident at Craigleith was frequently in charge of that institution prior to receiving a permanent appointment, while the lady resident at Craiglockhart was previously resident of a poorhouse in Scotland having sanctioned accommodation for 960 inmates; and in this connection, the Chairman had to point out that there were other poorhouses in Scotland for having hospitals attached thereto as large as, if not larger than, Craiglockhart, where the resident medical in charge was frequently a lady.

"Untrue statements"

Dr. Carmichael, Principal Medical Officer, reported with reference to the second paragraph of the letter dealing with the certification of the ailments from which the applicants suffered, that of 90 applicants certified during the month of March as suffering from rheumatism, only eight required hospital treatment. The fourth paragraph, which was put in inverted commas, and purported to be "what the Poor Law Commissioners reported" was the more serious. He realised that it was a grave matter to assert that statements made in what purported to be an extract from a Royal Commission were both misleading and untrue; but he would feel himself cowardly if he used milder terms when dealing with such a letter as Mr. Holland had sent. The report proceeded:

The untrue statements:

1. "The operations, some abdominal sections and others of apparent difficulty, were performed by the same one young lady doctor, with the help of a consultant who was a Physician". This is an utterly false statement as anyone having to do with the hospital can corroborate. The facts are the operations are done by myself, assisted either by the resident or an outside doctor, if required.

Should the operation be of a special character that I do not care to undertake, I have on several occasions got a surgical friend in the special line to operate, while I assisted. The statement that "the consultant was a physician" is misleading. If anyone cares to refer to the Medical Directory, it will be seen that my surgical appointments, qualifications and honours are more than those of an ordinary physician.

2. The report asserts the resident, "aided only by a consultant visiting twice a week"; the truth being, I am expected, and do go *thrice* a week, while I am at the call of the resident by telephone whenever she may wish to consult me or desire me out. Only 10 days ago, she called me out to operate on a strangulated hernia up at 10pm, the patient having been sent into the hospital that evening.

3. The report says there is 'a' phthisical ward; to be accurate, it should have said *three* phthisical wards and two open-air sheds.

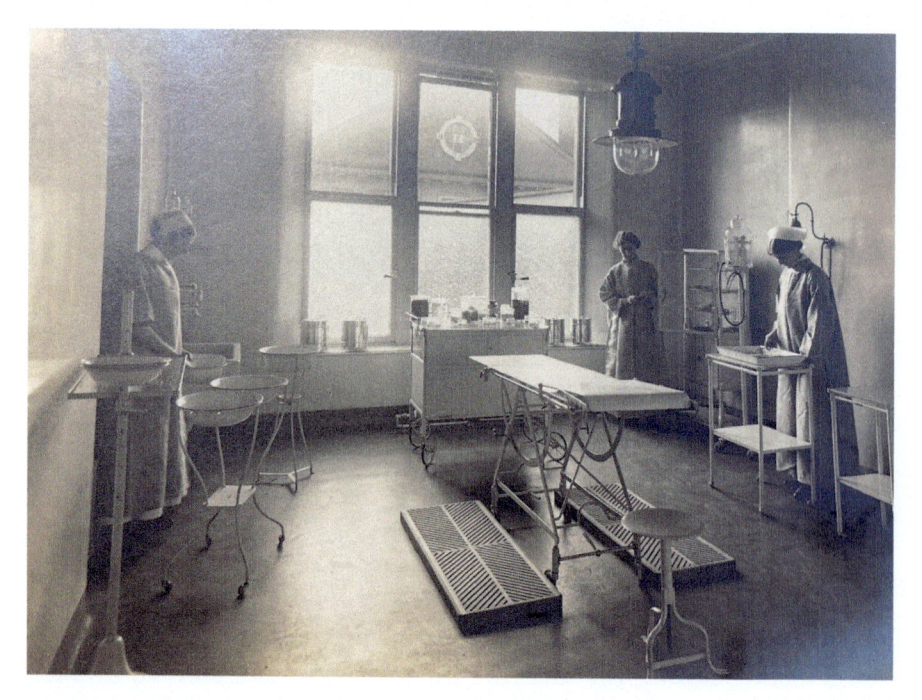

The "side room with one gas jet".

4. It adds "there is an ophthalmic ward". There is no such ward.

5. No record of the results is kept (referring to operations). While there is no casebook kept as in a general hospital, the bed charts, showing the progress and result of the case, are all kept and sent to the office, while the medical register shows a record of the operation and what the result.

A misleading letter

As to the misleading statements: The duties of the resident are detailed, but these are merely what are laid down by the Local Government Board and similar to all the poorhouses.

1. The report asserts the resident has to certify which of the adults – all presumably non able-bodied – were fit for work. Surely this does not take long for the few sent out each day; the misleading part of the statement "all presumably non able-bodied" being plain to those who know the work, as the great bulk suffer from minor ailments – 'footsore' 'pediculi' 'varicose veins' 'muscular rheumatism' and such ailments, which hardly makes the applicants non able-bodied. Then the resident has to settle the diet; but in such an institution there are regulation diets approved by the Local Government Board and all the resident has to do is to say "ordinary house diet", "milk diet", "mince" etc. and the dietary for that patient is at once understood.

2. Next it adds "extensive use is made of the pauper inmates". In my opinion is it is good for these inmates to have work to do; it helps them to improve in health matters much as is done in any convalescent home attached to a general hospital. Further, they do ward work, but not nursing proper.

3. "In many of the large wards that I entered, there were no trained nurses in attendance". Well, we have only 13 wards in all, and surely the nurse was present in some of the wards, as we have nine nurses for day duty and six for night, so surely the word 'many' used is too strong a term. With reference to Mr. Holland's own particular visit and report, it opened with a statement "on

the day after my visit she (the resident medical officer) was about to undertake, with the help of a very capable visiting physician, one of the most serious operations men can undergo". The statement was absolutely unwarranted, the President never being about to undertake such a responsibility.

A largely imaginary burden

Mr. Holland added there was no properly equipped operating room. Mr. Holland's mind was evidently imbued with the operating rooms in large surgical hospitals. Craiglockhart hospital was not counted a surgical hospital proper, while, of course, a certain amount of surgery required to be done. But had Mr. Holland never heard of the many operations that are constantly being done in bedrooms of private houses, quite as successfully, if not more so, than in hospitals with their operating theatres? If the Parish Council and the ratepayers desire to spend some hundreds of pounds in providing an operating room, then by all means let it be done. But if you put these patients on the same footing as that of patients in private practice and had them operated on in virtually a small bedroom, was he treating them badly? For the last 20 years he had operated in the side rooms with results, he was glad to say, no one needs to be ashamed of. It was not true as Mr. Holland asserted, that they were badly lighted. The light was all that could be desired by day. And with the one gas jet which Mr. Holland spoke of, Dr. Carmichael was able to operate comfortably on the strangulated hernia the other night from 10.30 to 11pm, with such success that the patient was dressed on the operating table, the symptoms all improved, and the wound not dressed again till the following week, when it was found healed and the stitches removed. Could any surgeon or Mr. Holland wish or expect a better result? There was a steriliser for the instruments, but none for the dressings. The reference to 42 patients being looked after by one nurse referred to the patients in one of the phthisis wards and the adjoining open-air shed, the latter requiring little or no nursing. Mr. Holland referred to "all" the post-mortems being done by the resident. The number varied much, being only undertaken in cases of sudden death of unknown cause or where there was difficulty in diagnosis. Probably six in the year was overstating the number. The whole strain of Mr. Holland's letter was misleading. The burden on the resident had been shown to be largely imaginary on Mr. Holland's part, but the resident liked it and did not feel it too much. She made no complaint of the work being too heavy. Although there were 280 patients in the hospital, possibly three quarters required no active medical or surgical treatment, but were simply chronic senile, nerve or rheumatic patients, requiring little else than nursing. The expressions of gratitude received from inmate after inmate, at one time taking the form of a 'round robin' from the inmates of a whole ward, were among the great lasting pleasures which Dr. Carmichael retains of the work he had had the privilege to do at the Poorhouse hospital.

The Resident Medical Officer's Report

The Resident Medical Officer, Craiglockhart, reported that she had been very much surprised at the statement made by Mr. Sydney Holland that, on the day after his visit, she was about to undertake, with the help of a consulting doctor, the most serious operation. She could not understand how Mr. Holland could have made such a statement, as she remembered distinctly saying, when asked by Mr. Holland whether she should herself undertake an emergency operation such as a strangulated hernia, that she should never dream of doing so. When asked what she would do in such cases, she said that she should immediately communicate with the visiting doctor, who would undertake the operation.

As a matter of fact, the operation referred to by Mr. Holland was performed by Dr. Carmichael with the assistance of another doctor, while she administered the anaesthetic. All operations had been done by Dr. Carmichael.

There were also read report by the Governors of Craiglockhart and Craigleith Poorhouses corroborating the statements by the medical officers. The former referring to Mrs. Webb's report, said he was surprised at some of her statements, as she expressed herself to the matron and head nurse as being well pleased with everything she had seen, and stated she had no idea everything was done so thoroughly. The Governor of Craigleith said he was afraid the charges against Craigleith made by Mr. Holland must have been given to Mrs. Sidney Webb by someone unauthorised party or by one who was ignorant of the conditions. He could not understand how any gentleman could do in half an-hour visit and then tear to pieces the management of a Scottish institution, the management being carried on by responsible citizens (assisted by a qualified officials) in the interests of the ratepayers and under the supervision and approval of the Local Government Board.

"Purely imaginary" shortcomings

The Chairman said it was unnecessary for him to deal *seriatim*[25] with the charges brought against the Council. In his opinion the most serious animadversion or allegation in the letter and report was that relating to operations at Craiglockhart. That animadversion the resident medical officer and principal medical officer had, to his mind, most effectually disposed of, and the reports of the doctors showed that as far as operations were concerned, the shortcomings alleged by Mr. Sydney Holland were purely imaginary. The vast majority of those in the hospitals only required good food and nursing at the hands of capable trained nurses, and the staff of trained nurses was at present, if anything, in excess of the Central Board's requirements. It was here where he thought considerable confusion of ideas took place. The name 'hospital' was misleading. The old name "sick wards" was much more truly applicable, but sentiment being strong, the name 'hospital' began to be applied to sick wards of poorhouses. During the last decade, there had been an increasing proportion of applicants for hospital relief, especially on the phthisical side and the House Committee had from time to time made provision to meet his tendency by the construction of special wards. They could all to some extent sympathise, the Chairman added, with the disappointment one accustomed to the palatial and expensively equipped theatres invariably associated with London hospitals, supported by endowments or charitable contributions, would feel when viewing the simple, yet thoroughly sanitary and hygienic methods in vogue in the Scottish poorhouses. As a Parish Council there were well aware of the many shortcomings of the present laws they had to administer. They had repeatedly and urgently, along with other councils in Scotland, brought the shortcomings under the notice of the powers

---

25   *Seriatim*: the handling of matters individually, rather than collectively.

Medical Care

that were, without success. In the meantime, pending legislation, which it was hoped would soon follow up on the report of the Poor Law Commission, they could assure Mr. Sydney Holland that the good people of Edinburgh are well aware that the Parish Council will continue to improve, modify or increase the institutions under their charge as may from time to time be deemed expedient to meet the requirements of the Parish. Several members of the committee expressed themselves in agreement that the Chairman's statement, but it was not considered necessary to adopt any resolution on the subject.

The Scotsman April 1912
Pauper help in hospitals.

The medical officers of Craiglockhart Poorhouse reported that they thought the time had come when the question of doing away altogether with pauper help in the wards, other than menial work, should be thoroughly gone into. They felt decidedly that sometimes the wards were unavoidably left to the care of paupers.

The sub-committee, having considered the matter, were of the opinion that the system of pauper help should be abolished, and a staff of probationers trained to assist the ward nurses should be engaged. The committee further agreed, in view of the recommendation regarding Craiglockhart Hospital, to recommend that the employment of inmates at Craigleith Hospital should also be abolished at the earliest opportunity. The House Committee however remitted the question back to the sub- committee to inquire as to the probable cost and to report.

The House Committee recommended that a second resident medical officer (male) be appointed for Craiglockhart Poorhouse, the reasons being the increased number of patients especially phthisis cases causing a large amount of bacteriological work, the great increase in surgical work and the teaching of probationers. The Council agreed the appointment should be made.

Dundee Courier October 1920
Outbreak of smallpox

An outbreak of smallpox has occurred at Craiglockhart Poorhouse near Edinburgh. Two women and four men all elderly being affected. None of them had been inoculated.

Edinburgh Evening News November 1920
Edinburgh Free of Smallpox

Dr Maxwell Williamson, the Medical Officer for Edinburgh announces today that Edinburgh is again free from smallpox. The isolation of the inmates of Craiglockhart Poorhouse, where some cases occurred, has been rigidly adhered to. The Poorhouse was disinfected and altogether 900 of the inmates, as well as the officials, were vaccinated. The patients who had been under treatment are now well, and one or two who are still in hospital will be discharged in a few days.

Scotsman June 1923
Open air treatment for young children

On the occasion of their visit to Craiglockhart Poorhouse Edinburgh, the members of the Edinburgh Women's Citizens Association were conducted on their first visit by the Governor Mr. Young over the section dealing with the normal poor. Dr. J W Keay, Principal Medical Officer, conducted the party on a second visit over the hospital. Dr. Keay pointed out that of the cases sent to hospital, 60% are acute and go out cured or greatly improved after treatment and able to return to work. He advocated strongly the need for an open-air life for the child, of sufficient nourishment and rest between the ages of one and fives, so liable to attack for example by the tubercle bacillus. The 100 beds of pale faced, sad little ones ought to be an inspiration to the women citizens of Edinburgh to see the Craiglockhart Poorhouse with its hospital receives its due share of financial support, so as to allow the beneficent and preventative work which is being done to be carried out to the best advantage.

Chapter 7
In Court

Edinburgh Evening News February 1875
The rheumatic pauper

At the Sheriff Summary Court this afternoon – Sheriff Gebbie on the bench – a man named Daniel Ross, lately an inmate of Craiglockhart Poorhouse, pleaded guilty to a charge of wilfully destroying a boot belonging to the parochial authorities by cutting a hole in it. The man stated that he had cut a hole in it in order to give his foot ease, as he was suffering from rheumatic pains. The Sheriff was informed however that this was not at all an uncommon practice in the Poorhouse. In consideration that the prisoner in this case was really suffering from the complaint stated, the Sheriff dismissed him with an admonition.

Edinburgh Evening News August 1885
Assault on a lunatic by his keeper

At Edinburgh Sheriff Court this afternoon – Sheriff Baxter presiding – Peter Reid, a middle-aged man, an attendant at Craiglockhart Poorhouse, pleaded guilty to having, on 8th inst., on the bank of the Union Canal near Sandyport, assaulted a male lunatic inmate of the Poorhouse by striking him on the back and buttocks with a walking stick. The Fiscal stated that at the time of the assault, the accused was out walking and had the man who was assaulted and others under his charge. The assaulted man jumped into the canal, but was rescued, and the accused took it upon himself to teach him a lesson. The Sheriff said the serious part of the offence consisted in the fact that the accused, being a person in charge of this lunatic, assaulted him. He (the Sheriff) had before him a doctor's certificate which showed that there was a bruise on the back part of the lunatic's person, although certainly not of a serious kind. These unfortunate creatures required to be treated with consideration and care, and the accused forgot that. He would have to pay a fine of £1 or suffer 10 days' imprisonment.

Edinburgh Evening News December 1899
Alleged assault at Craiglockhart

Monthly meeting of Edinburgh Parish Council was held today in the Council Chambers Castle Terrace, Mr Councillor Richard Clark presiding. In the minutes it was established that the subcommittee of the House Committee after inquiry had found that John Toolan, an inmate of Craiglockhart Poorhouse struck Hugh Jack the Labour Master a blow on the head with a woodchopper. The Labour Master, on his own admission after great provocation, struck Toolan on his being disarmed. The committee had failed to trace Toolan, who left the institution on the 30th. It was recommended that Mr Jack be cautioned and that in future should the occasion arise, the officials be instructed to bring the offenders before the Governor who shall have them locked up until the arrival of the police.

Edinburgh Evening News September 1899
A pauper's temptation

In Edinburgh Sheriff Summary Court today, Sheriff Maconochie on the bench, Thomas Mills, an elderly man, was sent to prison for 30 days for embezzling £1 3s 9d, the property of Edinburgh Parish Council on the 13th Inst. Mills was an inmate of Craiglockhart Poorhouse and was sent out to dispose of some firewood, however absconding with the proceeds. He had been four times previously convicted.

Edinburgh Evening News April 1874
Biting a man's leg

At the Sheriff Summary Court today before Sheriff Hallard, a man named James Brown was charged with assaulting on the 4th inst. an inmate of Craiglockhart Poorhouse by striking him several blows, forcing him down to the ground and biting part of his leg. He pleaded guilty and was sentenced to 10 days' imprisonment.

Edinburgh Evening News April 1878
Assault in a poorhouse

At the Edinburgh Sheriff Court yesterday, James Gourlay, an inmate of the Edinburgh City Poorhouse at Craiglockhart was charged with having assaulted a brother inmate, by striking him a severe blow in the breast. He pleaded guilty. It was stated that the prisoner had just been admitted into the house that day. The assaulted man was in charge of the bath and when the prisoner was taken to the bathroom, he continued smoking his pipe. The attendant asked him to give up his pipe and the prison replied by striking him. He was sent to prison for 10 days.

Edinburgh Evening News May 1904
Mean theft from Craiglockhart Poorhouse.

In Edinburgh Sheriff Court today Sheriff Guy sentenced a woman named Margaret Boswell to prison for 21 days for stealing a jacket and petticoat and a shawl from Craiglockhart Poorhouse. In sentencing her Sheriff Guy said that the theft was a mean one, she having gone into the Poorhouse and then stolen the articles. Boswell had been four times previously convicted.

The Scotsman 1930
Miner-tramp's turnip diet

"I have tramped from Wales looking for work, but I have not got any yet. At times are I was starving and had to live on turnips I took from fields" said an unemployed Cardiff man that when he appeared at Edinburgh Burgh Court yesterday, charged with lodging in a condemned house in Calton Road without the consent of the owners. On accused agreeing to work at Craiglockhart Poorhouse for some time, Baillie Gardner admonished him.

The Scotsman July 1922
A Police Court record holder

Mary Philbin or Auld (62) was convicted for the 297th time at Edinburgh City police court yesterday. Auld, whose address was given as Craiglockhart Poorhouse, admitted to having been found drunk and incapable on Tuesday in the North Meadow Walk. She had been convicted on the same charge 228 times previously. The public prosecutor Mr. MacPherson said he thought the woman had a record number of convictions for the court. In imposing a fine of £2.00- or 20-days Baillie Bathgate advised Auld to go back to the Poorhouse and stay there.

The East Aberdeenshire Observer October 1889
New Deer
Arrival of an old Edinburgh Offender

Jane Kirk, who has been convicted over 300 times in Edinburgh of drunkenness and minor offences such as a breach of the peace, left Edinburgh on Friday for a croft in New Deer where she has to reside. Baillie Walcott has been the means of getting her home. She is to be kept by a worthy couple in a croft in New Deer, where the nearest public house is over 7 miles distant. It is hoped she will gradually lose her almost insatiable desire for liquor. For the past fortnight – or rather since she last broke out, she has been accommodated in the Craiglockhart Poorhouse and seemed quite pleased by the prospect of leaving the city. Before starting out on her journey, Jane was fully rigged and looked quite a changed individual. Her finery she owes to the efforts of Miss Walcott, who it seems has visited her on one or two occasions. The Bailie has received a few subscriptions towards the fund for defraying the cost of reclaiming Jane. From one publican he received a donation of £5.00, accompanied by a very sympathetic letter which Bailie Walcot appreciated very much. Jane has been sent to Aberdeen in charge of a man who will not return until she is quite established in her new home.

May 1917 Mid Lothian Advertiser
Stealing bones

Two men named Alexander and George Campbell were each sentenced at Edinburgh Sheriff Court to two months imprisonment for stealing five cwt of bones from Craiglockhart Poorhouse.

Edinburgh Evening News 1876
Assault in Craiglockhart Poorhouse

At the Edinburgh Sheriff Summary Court yesterday afternoon P Ronaghan, an inmate of Craiglockhart Poorhouse, was charged with assaulting a fellow inmate named Peter Roy. While in bed on the 25th inst. the parties got into a discussion about Irish affairs. Ronaghan apparently had the worst of the argument and thought he would soothe his wounded dignity by thrashing Roy. He got up, pulled him out of bed, jumped upon his chest and otherwise maltreated him. Before the magistrate, the prisoner was in a repentant mood. He pleaded guilty and was sentenced to 60 days imprisonment with hard labour.

The Courier Christmas Day 1919
Baby left outside poorhouse.

The story of how a young mother abandoned for three weeks old child was told to the Edinburgh Sheriff Court yesterday. The mother, a respectably dressed girl of 19 admitted the offence and also that she had falsely registered the child, which was illegitimate and was born in the Hospice 219 High Street Edinburgh.

The Prosecutor explained that after the birth, the girl was removed from the Hospice to Craiglockhart Poorhouse, but she wished to be allowed away. She was refused at first but two days afterwards, she was allowed to go. She took the child with her and going along the avenue towards the main road she appears to have put the child down at the side of the walk where there is a small grass footpath and a number of trees.

The Right Course

About half an hour afterwards one of the officials of the Poorhouse was walking along the avenue when he saw a child. It was sound asleep. He did not know whose it was but when it was taken back to the Poorhouse, the child was recognised at once as that of the girl who had just left. The child was well wrapped up and had not received any injury.

Addressing the girl, Sheriff MacLeod said one could appreciate her distressful condition and seeing that she had been imprisoned for a short time pending the hearing of her case, he thought the ends of justice would be met by an admonition. He understood that the girl's mother who was in court was willing to take her home, and he hoped the future would show he had taken the right course.

Edinburgh Evening News October 1874
Child Desertion

At the Sheriff Summary Court on Saturday a woman named Mary McLaughlin was charged at the instance of the Inspector of Poor to the Parish of Colinton with deserting her child. In June she was an inmate of the Craiglockhart Poorhouse from which he escaped by scaling the wall and left her child behind. No trace of her could be found until Saturday, when she was captured at Lennie's Port. The accused stated that she was willing to take possession of a child. She was ordered to pay £2.00 nine shillings, the amount which the Parish had expended on the child or be imprisoned for 24 hours.

Edinburgh Evening News May 1895[26]
Alleged Child Murder at Craiglockhart Poorhouse

Alice Turnbull, an attendant in the lunatic ward at Craiglockhart Poorhouse, appeared before Sheriff Hamilton in Edinburgh Sheriff Court today, and emitted a declaration on a charge of murdering her illegitimate new-born child in the Poorhouse on 20 April.

---

26 This Edinburgh Evening News page has a notable first line "Oscar Wilde is suffering from nervous prostration".

Edinburgh Evening News 13th May 1895
Lunatic Attendant sent to prison.

A respectable-looking woman, named Alice Turnbull, 27 years of age, was sentenced by Sheriff Blair in Edinburgh Sheriff Criminal Court today, to four months' imprisonment for concealment of pregnancy. Mr David Murray stated that hitherto the accused had been a good character as a domestic servant. She got into the company of a man who had promised to marry her, but that promise had not been fulfilled. Consequently in her condition she became depressed in spirits. She did not expect to be confined so soon, and she became unconscious and therefore unable to call for assistance. It was a pity, the agent said, that the law could not reach the seducer of innocent girls as well as the girls themselves. The Sheriff said the accused had pleaded guilty to concealment, and he would have to take it that she did not call for assistance. Mr Blane, the Depute-Fiscal, stated that the child was found dead in bed, suffocated by the bed-clothes. In passing sentence, the Sheriff said he had considered all the circumstances. The accused, it appears, had been in the employment of the Parochial Authorities scarcely three weeks, and had discharged the duties of lunatic attendant.

Edinburgh Evening News July 1932
An artful old lady. The lady vanishes.

One habitual drunkard who achieved such unhappy distinction week or two ago, quite contentedly chatted with Baillie Andrew Young on the comparative conditions of life in Barlinnie Prison Glasgow and Saughton Prison[27]. He had lived in both and preferred Saughton because it was furnished with a wooden floor! He was quite content, he admitted, making his home in Saughton and did not seem the least concerned about the Baillie's suggestions that a "permanent home" should be found for him. Such is the outlook of the incorrigible. There are the others who hang their heads with shame in the dock and who in most cases are happy to take full advantage of an admonition. Then there are others who pose in the dock and whose acting as

---

27   Saughton Prison in Edinburgh

often as bad as their court records. One of these artful offenders, an elderly woman succeeded with a plausible tale and a tearful appeal. Instead of sending her to prison for getting drunk, the Bailie was quite pleased to exact a promise that she would go and stay in Craiglockhart Poorhouse. If she did not go to Craiglockhart, she was warned, she would be taken back to the court and very severely punished. The lady was shocked! *"If I don't go to Craiglockhart,"* she said, *"I would deserve to be punished"*. Enquiries showed that she did deserve to be punished. The lady vanished! The next time there was a similar appeal to the Baillie, the treatment was more certain.

Edinburgh Evening News July 1874
Alleged house breaking at Craiglockhart Poorhouse.

Two men, named respectively Thomas Heriot and Cuthbert Short, the former of whom is a returned convict, have been apprehended and examined by the Sheriff on a charge of breaking into Craiglockhart Poorhouse and abstracting a number of articles of clothing on the 21st or 22nd of this month. Short was apprehended yesterday morning by the City Police with the stolen articles in his possession and was taken before Sheriff Hamilton at the City Police Court, who granted warrant for his detention on the ground that he had articles in his possession which were supposed to have been stolen or otherwise unlawfully come by. Information was lodged with the County Police and Constable Forbes of Slateford, on making investigations, found that the storehouse at Craiglockhart had been forcibly entered by the windows and several articles of clothing stolen. Both prisoners were remitted for further examination

Evening Telegraph December 1922
Scene in an Edinburgh Poorhouse
Governor attacked with heavy stick.

In connection with a wild outburst of temper in the Craiglockhart Poorhouse Edinburgh John Dalton (20) a shoemaker, was sent to prison for 20 days at Edinburgh Police Court today

Dawson one morning recently refused to get up for breakfast and also refused to carry out his usual routine. The Governor ordered him to his work and he immediately became disorderly, striking one of the labour masters a severe blow on the right ear. He was immediately set upon by three men and taken to a cell. He was not long in however when he managed to wrench off the iron lock and rushing out with a heavy stick, hit the Governor over the knee to the effusion of blood. A previous conviction for assault was libelled against the accused, who is very deaf.

Dundee Courier and Advertiser July 1931
Poorhouse Governor sent to prison.

Sentence of eight months imprisonment was passed by Sheriff Brown at Edinburgh Sheriff Court yesterday on William Young, former Governor of Craiglockhart Poorhouse Edinburgh, for having, while in the employment of Edinburgh Parish Council, embezzled between 15th of May 1924 and 15th May 1930 a sum of £915 three shillings and three pence.

Mr RP Morrison advocate on behalf of the accused said Young was 51 years of age and a married man. Apart from the circumstances of this case, he had a long and honourable record of public service. He was appointed Assistant Governor of Craiglockhart Poorhouse in 1903 and held that position for six years when he was appointed Governor, a position he maintained until November 1930. Unfortunately, during the years mentioned in the indictment what was at first carelessness in failing to account for certain monies connected with a piggery developed into criminal carelessness to finally come within reach of the criminal law.

Lived modestly.

The accused had always lived modestly but in the past few years obligations of a family nature had caused a drain on his resources.

Sheriff Brown- *How long have these deficiencies gone on for so long unobserved?*

Mr W Horn, Procurator Fiscal, said that a book was kept at the Poorhouse, in which there was a record of the pigs in the piggery.

By suppression of the fact that there were more pigs than there were entered in the books, the deficiencies had arisen.

Sheriff Brown passed sentence as stated.

The same case was also reported in the Dundee Evening Telegraph January 1931
Ex Official sent to prison.
Former Governor of Poorhouse
Edinburgh man's downfall

At Edinburgh Sheriff Court today Sheriff Brown sent William Young for ex-Governor of the Craiglockhart Poorhouse to eight months imprisonment for embezzlement. Young, who was for many years the Governor of the Poorhouse was arrested in Newcastle. He pleaded guilty to a charge. On behalf of the accused, counsel said he was aged 51 and a married man. Apart from the circumstances of this case, he had a long and honourable record of public service.

He was appointed assistant governor of Craiglockhart Poorhouse in 1903 and held that position for six years, when he was appointed Governor a position he maintained until November 7, 1930.

He had many responsible duties in connection with these two posts, there being over 1000 people receiving care at the institution under his charge.

For nearly 30 years he had satisfied the public authorities and the persons under his care as an efficient governor and a man who was humane and kindly in the treatment of the people in the institution.

Sent to prison.

Unfortunately, carelessness in failing to account for certain monies connected with a piggery developed into criminal carelessness to eventually come within the reach of the criminal law.

The judge- *"How have these deficiencies gone on for so long unobserved?"*

In Court

Counsel "-there is no doubt the books of the institution were perfectly kept and audited butt it was in a separate book relating to the piggery that the offence took place. The accused himself was at a loss to know how the shortage was never discovered. The amount involved was £950.

Sheriff Brown said that the accused had such a position of trust it was impossible for him to take other than a very serious view of the case. On the other hand, he felt some weight was due to the consideration put forward on the accused's behalf. Previous good character would also have to be taken into consideration. On balancing these matters, the Sheriff said he would impose a sentence of eight months imprisonment.

Edinburgh Evening News July 1877
Recovery although of lost child

The little fellow about five years of age, son of Mr. George Alexander Bangor Road Leith disappeared eight days ago, and it was conjectured that he had been abducted by a female itinerant hawker. The police were put on her track. Yesterday however the boy was discovered in Craiglockhart Poorhouse and was returned to his parents, who since the time of his disappearance had been in a state of much distress.

The Peoples Journal May 1930
Novel Coining Offence
Half-crowns made in Poorhouse.
The capture

Finding time hanging heavily on his hands, Peter Forbes Wilson (30) an inmate of Craiglockhart Poorhouse Edinburgh devoted his leisure hours to the manufacture of counterfeit coins.

His activities did not remain unchecked for long, for the coins he produced by these illicit methods were detected by the authorities of the institution.

Retribution was swift and resulted in the appearance of Wilson at the Sheriff Court, where two charges of contravention of the Coining Act were made against him.

The first charge bore that on 14th of April in Craiglockhart Poorhouse, he had in his possession a mould adapted and intended to impress the likeness of both sides of a half-crown piece, and the second charge was that between 27 November 1929 and 14 April 1930 he made or counterfeited 10 coins to resemble or pass for half-crown pieces.

Wilson, who had four previous convictions, pleaded guilty and was sentenced by Sheriff Principal Brown to four months' imprisonment.

The Governor of the Poorhouse had been aware for some weeks that the counterfeit coins had been circulated in the institution and he made enquiries amongst the inmates regarding the matter. These counterfeit coins were said to resemble florins and sixpences.

Within the institution is a store where inmates can purchase cigarettes during certain hours of the day. A 76-year-old inmate is in charge of this store and during the month past he had found 3 counterfeit coins amongst his drawings. The old man's sight is not very good, and he could not say who had given him these coins.

Walking mint

One morning the Governor received information that Wilson was making counterfeit coins and had a mould for the purpose in his possession. Wilson became an inmate in the institution in November 1929, and since his admission he had been employed as a warder in a hospital ward. Immediately the Governor secured the information regarding Wilson, he informed the police.

The Governor, accompanied by two detectives, proceeded to the ward where Wilson was employed. The officers informed Wilson that they had information that he had been making counterfeit coins. Wilson denied all knowledge of the matter and a search was made of his clothing.

In his jacket pocket was found a mould, wrapped up in a piece of newspaper, which showed the impression of both sides of a half-crown piece. Wrapped in a handkerchief in another pocket of his jacket were seven counterfeit coins resembling half-crowns which were poorly manufactured and had the appearance of being taken from the mould.

In a small pocket at the top of his trousers were three more counterfeit coins also resembling half-crowns These coins had been filed and polished and were evidently complete ready for passing off.

In other pockets of Wilson's clothing were found seven small pieces of metal, the metal top of a syphon bottle, a regimental cap badge. These articles were of a type suitable for melting and making into counterfeit coins.

A file was also found in one of Wilson's pockets. It bore white marks showing that it had probably been used for dressing the counterfeit coins. A metal spoon found in another pocket was burned and blackened and had evidently been used to melt the ingredients for the coins. From a spot on the bottom of the spoon, it appeared to have been used over the burner in the kitchen fire where Wilson worked.

A small metal goblet was found on the kitchen floor which bore traces of molten white metal on the bottom inside. This might also have been used for melting purposes.

The counterfeit florins passed in the cigarette store of the institution, which were handed over to the detectives, appeared to be of identical composition to the counterfeit coins in Wilson's possession. All were of very coarse manufacture.

Accused's explanation

An agent on Wilson's behalf said that whilst in the Poorhouse in February of this year, Wilson found three moulds and 12 coins in a box on the verandah there. Since he found them, he had been experimenting with the coins. He had melted down the coins and tried to make new coins with the aid of the moulds and by this method actually made three coins. He eventually destroyed two of the moulds and retained one.

Wilson stated that his handling of the moulds was only an experiment and he had no intention of uttering coins; it was merely something for him to do and he never thought that the coins he produced would pass for real.

Wilson made no attempt to conceal his activities, for he had shown the coins to several people in the Poorhouse and the moulds were left lying about in the kitchen.

The Fiscal, Mr W Horn, stated that the base coins were passed in the canteen shortly after Wilson went into the Poorhouse. The moulds and coins were certainly crude, but the latter were good enough to deceive an old storekeeper.

Sheriff Brown said he could not accept the explanation offered that Wilson's offence was only an interesting experiment, for in so doing, all guilt would be taken out of the matter. In point of fact Wilson had passed one or two coins and the offence was a serious one. The accused had a bad previous record, and he would impose sentence of four months imprisonment.

Chapter 8

The Catholic Priest's Cab Fare

This tale of argument over expenses reflects the attempts of the Poorhouse Authorities to protect the position of the Church of Scotland against incursions from other denominations.

Edinburgh Evening News September 1877

The Rev. Mr. Hannan[28] moved the motion of which he had given notice:

"That the expenses of the clergymen who minister to the spiritual wants of the Catholic inmates in the Craiglockhart Poorhouse be paid by this Board".

In doing so he explained that it was only the expenses of one clergyman he wished paid and, by expenses he did not mean a salary, but simply the hire of a cab to convey him out to the Poorhouse once a week. Mr. Councillor Buchanan seconded the motion. The demands to pay Mr. Hannan's clergyman had been put him in a very beautiful way indeed. For it was merely the expense of a cab. This was merely the thin end of the wedge. If the demand were granted, they would have Mr. Chinnery[29] and the other clergymen applying for the same privilege and where would it all end? Mr. Officer said they had acknowledged the claims of the Roman Catholic portion of the inmates of the Poorhouse for separate religious instruction, and surely it would not be a great stretch of principle to pay the expense of a cab for the Roman Catholic clergyman? Mr. Lewis said that out of the 553 inmates of the Poorhouse, only 135 when Roman Catholics. Excluding these and the Presbyterian sections of the inmates, there

---

28 Priest in Charge, St Patrick's RC Church in the Cowgate, an area known as 'Little Ireland'
29 The Episcopalian Curate of All Souls, soon to feature in the tale of Miss Weir Chapter 10

were nine separate sects in the Poorhouse. If they granted Mr. Hannan's application, they would be surrounded by numbers of every kind. After some further discussion, a vote was taken between the two motions. 12 voted for each, and the Chairman giving his casting motion in favour of Mr. Hannan's motion, it was declared carried.

At a meeting of the Edinburgh City Parochial Board on Monday it was resolved by 15 votes to six to rescind the resolution to grant £10 a year for the Roman Catholic priest to visit the Craiglockhart Poorhouse.

The Freemans Journal Dublin October 1877

He is an uneducated man whoever does not know that the Scottish Reformation Society is one of the most famous organisations in Christendom and he is an unwise man whoever does not understand that it is meritorious as it is renowned, that it carries its prerogative with it, and that if it only had power as it had authority, it would absolutely govern the world. The SRS justifies its existence and signalises its usefulness from time to time by brilliant epiphanies, as it did notably a couple of days ago in its magnanimous deliverance regarding the Rev. Mr. Hannan's cab fare, which we mentioned on Thursday. As a reader will remember, the *fons et origo mali*[30] was this. They have in Edinburgh a poorhouse and in the poorhouse 135 Catholic inmates. Edinburgh is a great deal too religious to make any sort of religious provision for these Papist pariahs and what Edinburgh did not do for these poor people, one of the Catholic priests of the city did. The Rev. Mr. Hannan has been in the habit of affording spiritual ministrations to his coreligionists in the poorhouse gratuitously, and last week the guardians were considerate enough to allow this gentleman a cab to convey him to the place where he spends his unremunerated labour on their own sick poor. As soon as the Scottish Reformation Society became aware of this backsliding and degenerate proceeding, they lost no time in sounding the tocsin[31] and they issued a manifesto declaring that day "*have observed with astonishment that the managers of the poor for the City of Edinburgh*

---

30 Lat." The source and origin of the evil"
31 An alarm bell (from 14C French)

have resolved by the casting vote of their Chairman to place a carriage at the disposal of the Popish Priest who visits the workhouse inmates" They pronounce the decision of the Board "an offensive and infatuated resolution for which the ratepayers ought to get rescinded" and they add that "the increasing insidious and insatiable demands the Romish priests in this country call for the firmest resistance". This objection to the indulgence granted to that "insidious and insatiable" man professes to be based on religious principle and on the never dying duty of opposing Popery at all points. Its efficiency in this respect may be a matter of question and at all events one who knows anything of the present religious distractions of Scotland would suppose that the Presbyterians might find quite enough of occupation inside own household of faith, without giving need to the religious concerns of other people.

With their three Presbyterian nominations at war with each other and at war within themselves; with their "tabled libels" against the Revs. Dr. Dod, Robertson Smith and Macrea; with their various mutinies against the Standards of Faith; with their disputes and dodgeries about State pay; with the scandal of the Government subsidy in Madras; and with the apparent die out of religion amongst all sections of their people, they had better be mending their nets and repairing their breaches than playing dog in a manger with their neighbours. Granting a cab drive to a minister will not revivify Calvinism and refusing it to a "Popish Priest" will not kill Popery in Scotland. Besides if this principle is not encouraging the "insidious demands" of the terrible Papists be sound and right, it ought not to stop at stopping a cab. The Scottish Reformation Society ought to have the courage of their convictions and to carry out the convictions consistently. Is it not encouraging Popery to allow the papers in the Poorhouse to have food, raiment and lodging at the expense of the ratepayers? Is it not that making the ratepayers partake of the sin of Popery? And is it not a crime against God and conscience to pay a doctor to attend and cure these Papists? In fact, if these things are not national sins, we cannot imagine what a national sin can be. While these crimes are tolerated, 'tis vain to murmur about a cab, and if the cab is to be suppressed on the score of aggrieved conscience, so Papists and Popery everywhere in Scotland be suppressed. But it is not religious principle alone which the SRS assigns for its

Father Edward Hannan 1836-1891.

Did much to help the condition of Catholics in Edinburgh. Founder, first manager and president of Hibernian Football Club est. 1875.

opposition to the laxity of the board, and they proceed to throw in economic considerations. The carriage placed at the disposal of the Popish Priest is so placed, they say, at the expense of the ratepayers as often as he (the Popish Priest) chooses to visit the Popish inmates of the workhouse; and then they go on to state that, "*this concession may imply a very large outlay, as the "number of such visits may become indefinitely great*". This "very large outlay" in the cab of an" insatiable priest "would manifestly bankrupt Edinburgh; and while the proper custodians of the rates are slumbering and sleeping, and letting the city be ruined, the Reformation Society, adding this duty to its other labours, guards the capitol. Does Edinburgh at all know the depth and extent of her indebtedness to his amiable and charitable confraternity? Has she it in her power to rewarded in any adequate measure? What would she do, were it not for this insatiably great and good organisation? And what is to be said of the Board that, even by a casting vote, incurred the grave displeasure of such a society? The thought makes as shudder, as the inevitable perdition which they so obstinately wooed rises before our minds. To think that the "odd man" on a public board should have such an evil disposition and should have so much in his power! It is too bad; and even this is not all. "*The endowment of Popery*" says the society, "*tends to the subversion of the Reformation and of the Constitution and liberties of the country*". We often heard a great event springing from trifling causes; but never before imagined that a priest's poorhouse cab hire involved no less disasters and the smash-up of the Reformation and the collapse of the glorious British Constitution?

The Reverend Canon Hannan appears again in the newspapers in connection with a financial issue, as the *Edinburgh Evening News* of March 1889 showed:

Edinburgh Catholics and Canon Hannan

A meeting of Catholics "*to express sympathy with Canon Hannan in his recent great loss through the absconding of the late secretary of the Yearly Society, Mr John McFadden, and to make arrangements for a general subscription to indemnify the Rev. gentleman as far as possible*" was held in St Mary's Hall last night – Mr M Flannigan presided. Mr D Donworth, who had examined the books of the society, stated that he found the deficiency to be about £360 or £361. The branch that closed a few weeks ago had been paid to the extent of £262 and in the branch that would close in September there was a deficiency of about £100, which sum, of course, Canon Hannan was also prepared to meet in due time. The Chairman expressed sympathy with Mr McFadden's family and said that he believed a letter had been received from Mr McFadden, who had gone to America, which stated that, if spared in health, he might yet be able to make up all the deficiency which had occurred in connection with that society. The following resolution was then passed *"That this meeting, having heard the report of Mr Donworth regarding the amount of the deficiency in the funds of the Yearly Society, and which has been met in the most honourable manner by the Treasurer, Canon Hannan, tenders the Rev. gentleman its deep sympathy in the unfortunate position in which he is placed and pledges itself to indemnify him as far as possible for the great loss he has sustained".* Upwards of £23 had been received towards the object of the meeting.

Chapter 9
Eternal Damnation

A touching tale of the dismissal of the Poorhouse Chaplain, the Reverend Horace Smith, whose preaching strayed from the orthodox, gives us a vivid insight into the influence of religion on the administration of the Poorhouse and tensions within Scottish society in the 1880s. This case made the newspapers throughout Britain and Ireland; much of the reporting was sympathetic, as shown by this rhyme in the Dundee Courier of 31st December 1883.

TO THE EDINBURGH CHAPLAIN

Alas! Poor Smith, your daily bread
You've foolishly forfeited.
The place of woe you can't forego
And yet be kindly treated.
Your Christian Board, who fear the Lord
Must need correct your error.
Whate'er your fate in future state
You've here a reign of terror.
Your pauper flock must bear the shock
Of earthly separation
You're sacrificed, without a doubt,
To work out their salvation

J.

Heresy hunt in a Poorhouse

Glasgow Herald November 1883
Edinburgh Parochial Board and their chaplain

A special meeting of Edinburgh City Parochial Board was held yesterday to receive a report from the House Committee on a letter from Mr HW Smith, chaplain of Craiglockhart Poorhouse, which was remitted by the board to the House Committee at last meeting. That letter was brought under the notice of the Board but only a sentence of it was then read when the Chairman said It should be at once remitted to the House Committee, which was done. The House Committee now reported:

"That in view of the opinion stated by Mr Smith in the letter now read the board dispenses with his services" This motion has been adopted by the Committee by 13 to three in favour of requiring Mr Smith to refrain from teaching such matters as were contained in his letter and which were contrary to the obligations he undertook at his appointment, and that if he still persisted in teaching such doctrines, he must either resign or be dismissed. In view of their decision the Committee had suspended Mr Smith. Mr McKnight, advocate, at yesterday's meeting moved the approval of the Committee's recommendation. Mr Towert seconded.

Councillor Tate said that the House Committee had been in a very great hurry and had adopted a very summary modent procedure in settling this matter as they had done. It was not becoming to the Board to be so hurried and they ought to have had more consideration for the interests at stake. No Kirk Session, Presbytery or other body accustomed to judge in matters of this kind would have so acted, and more time and thought were required in a matter of this kind, especially nowadays when they were getting lighter and when their views on many subjects were being changed or modified. Mr Smith's offence was that he had doubts about or denied the doctrine of Eternal Punishment.

Mr Towert – *"more than that"*

Councillor Tate said he would not say whether Mr Smith was right or wrong. He was not he thought qualified to judge of that, but he knew there was a large section of Christian people who held the same views as Mr Smith held and the question was, was this heresy or error? If it was as bald as a Christian doctrine by others, it might turn out to be no heresy at all. Most of them had been taught and up till recently believed that the world was created in six days. Now he believed it was satisfactorily proved that the work occupied for very much longer time.

Mr McKnight – *"no"*

Councillor Tate said that he would excuse his learned friend, but other people's views on the point were now very much modified. Again, they had all been taught when they were younger there was a place where the good went and a place where all the bad went, which literally burned with fire and brimstone. Upon that views were now very much modified. He then showed how all the church in Galileo's day had been wrong and had persecuted him for belief in the earth's motion, yet Galileo was right and all the church wrong. Not 50 years ago there was a controversy about the Atonement[32], and many were turned out of the church, yet now the large body of Christians had come round and adopted those views (cries of *"no"* and *"never"*) which caused Baillie Cranston[33] and Councillor McDougall to protest against the interruptions and demand a fair hearing for Councillor Tate. Councillor Tate resuming said that this Board was going on the very same principle as one that prevailed in Scotland when people who dared to differ with the powers that were, were hunted down and taken to the stake or the gibbet. In this case the Board were not persecuting to the death, but they were prosecuting notwithstanding, because they were using their powers to persecute this man with his wife and family, turning them out of the house and out of their means of subsistence. He was greatly mistaken if the people of Edinburgh or of Scotland would like an action of this kind performed

---

32 In 1856 the Rev John Mcleod Campbell published a work questioning whether Christ had to die to effect atonement for Man's sins. This departure from 'official' theory profoundly influenced Scottish theology.

33 Bailie Robert Cranston 1815-1892. Founder of the Waverley Temperance Hotels.

by City Parochial Board. He moved that *"this Board does not approve of the Committee's report but requests the chaplain to attend to the conscientious discharge of his duties and ministering to the poor and not to communicate to this board any point of Christian doctrine which may cause him perplexity".*

Mr Gowans said he had received a letter, which had not yet read, from the Chaplain who'd asked him to read it before the Board. Several objections were raised on the ground that the letter was not addressed to the Board and it was ultimately agreed to hear Baillie Cranston. Before reading the letter, Baillie Cranston said it was the strangest thing that had ever happened to the Board to be asked to adopt the report without ever having heard the letter of Mr Smith read. The Committee had tried and condemned the man without the document on which he had been tried having been laid before this Board.

Mr Lewis said it was read at the meeting.

Baillie Cranston replied that the Chairman very properly, no doubt, stopped the reading of the letter at the Board; but it never had been read at the Board, nor had the substance of it even being given. Instead of bringing the letter to the Board and the reasons for their decision upon it, the Committee had told the man he was suspended. There was difference in the Board as the Committee now would see upon this question. He believed the clergymen themselves had given up quarrelling about it, and he thought a general committee including the House Committee should be appointed to take the subject into serious consideration and the matter should be thoroughly discussed before they asked the Board to put this man away. No respectable minister now ever preached torture in hell fire. That belonged to the days of 300 years ago. But this poor man was to suffer for his views. He liked Mr. Smith – he had not thought there was much philosophy in Mr. Smith before – but when he heard what Mr. Smith was teaching to the poor people, he himself thought that, to people in that position, the least they could do was to send them all to Heaven; and he thought Mr. Smith was rendering a great service when he abolished Hell for them. He therefore thought the Board should be very thankful. There was another thing which Mr. Smith said, and said truly, that eternal torture was not compatible with the power of the love of God ("*hear hear*") with the words 'love' and 'eternal goodness' and wisdom and all that belonged to the attributes of God were not compatible with eternal torture, which meant no relief or no change. Now the punishments given in the world was given with two distinct ideas -for the protection of society and for the reformation of the criminal. But if a man was to be sent to Hell, it did not matter what then- for there was no remedy. The Chaplin said that this was not compatible with God's mighty love and wisdom and goodness and therefore he preached to the poor people.

The Northern Chronicle January 1884

Probably the unfortunates in Craiglockhart Poorhouse felt grateful to the Chaplain of the institution for preaching to them for the new doctrine of universal salvation and no eternal punishment[34]. At any rate the Governor of the establishment who, in his position and surroundings may possibly be a little Pharisaical, was the only informer against the Chaplain's departure from the fundamental doctrines of the church. The chaplain seems also to have written informing the Board of the changes in his religious conceptions and generously offering, in a specified number of discourses, to bring the members of the said Board to his own peculiar way of thinking. Of course, the Board declined; and the Chaplain, being advised of consequences that might ensue, speedily retracted and again withdrew himself within the limits of orthodoxy. Unfortunately, however, being convinced against his will, he remained of the same opinion still and was honest enough to acknowledge as much. The Parochial Board in question, that of the City of Edinburgh, has just resolved to free the Chaplain from his embarrassing position by dismissal. The opinion almost unanimously prevailed at the Board that, however acceptable the doctrine of universal happiness hereafter may be to the poor and unfortunate who inhabit the Poorhouse, they should be taught to regard these matters in the light of the Bible, as all wise people do. There was one member

---

[34] Bering predestined to eternal punishment in Hell. The Calvinistic belief that God appoints the eternal destiny of some to salvation, while others receive eternal damnation for their sins.

who confessed that he held the Chaplain's view of the question and brought forward the name of his minister as approver; but while this may prove that the subject of eternal punishment is, as everybody knows, one of controversy. It is no reason why paupers should have their worldly cares increased by heterodoxical teaching.

A Scotch Parochial Board could not have acted otherwise than this board has done, whatever latitudinarians[35] may have to say.

The Truth February 1884

I mentioned the other day that the Edinburgh Parochial Board had dismissed the Chaplain of Craiglockhart Poorhouse so because he had refused to preach the doctrine of eternal punishment to the inmates. The unfortunate man for having a wife and family and being dependent on his salary formally recanted his obnoxious views and solemnly promised to preach and teach such "simple Gospel truths as the managers may deem most suitable". He humbled himself in vain; but he might have known that to forgive the prostrate enemy is not in the nature of an austere Presbyterian. He was sent about his business in spite of his 14 years services. But for his very foolish recantation he might possibly have made a good thing out of his martyrdom. The salary of the post is 130 pounds a year with apartments, coals and gas. There are no fewer than 48 applicants for it, including 10 ministers ,12 missionaries, nine teachers, eight divinity students, a gardener, four small merchants and a retired Major of Dragoons.

Evening News and Star January 1884

A few weeks ago, I alluded to the strange proceedings of the Edinburgh Parochial Board which had threatened to dismiss the Chaplain at Craiglockhart Poorhouse, because he declined to preach the doctrine of eternal punishment. Last Thursday the members met to decide the matter and after reading the Chaplain's explanations,

---

35 Latitudinarians were originally 17C theologians from Cambridge University who were moderate Anglicans. The term was later used to categorise churchmen who depended on reason, rather than tradition, for moral certainty.

it was resolved by a small majority to dismiss him. His letter setting forth his views was denounced by one pillar of orthodoxy as a most ridiculous and contemptible composition which could never have come from any man of prudence or sound theological learning. The more sensible minority were in favour of instructing the Chaplain to attend conscientiously to the ministration of the poor and to refrain from subjects of an irritating and controversial nature. One of his supporters announced that two celebrated ministers in the city had reported that the Chaplain's views were not of a nature to justify his dismissal, a statement which was met by cries of "horrible" and "shameful". The Scotch still have a keen scent for a heresy hunt, their inveterate bigotry cannot be stamped out in the meridian of Auld Reekie.

Glasgow Herald November 1883
Heresy hunt in a Poorhouse
Edinburgh Parochial Board and their chaplain

A special meeting of Edinburgh City Parochial Board was held yesterday to receive a report from the House Committee on a letter from Mr HW Smith chaplain of Craiglockhart Poorhouse which was remitted by the board to the House Committee at last meeting. That letter was brought under the notice of the Board, but only a sentence of it was then read when the chairman said It should be at once remitted to the House Committee, which was done. The House Committee now reported:

"That in view of the opinion stated by Mr Smith in the letter now read the board dispenses with his services" This motion has been adopted by the committee by 13 to 3 in favour of requiring Mr Smith to refrain from teaching such matters as were contained in his letter and which were contrary to the obligations he undertook at his appointment, and that if he still persisted in teaching such doctrines he must either resign or be dismissed. In view of their decision the committee had suspended Mr Smith. Mr McKnight advocate at yesterday's meeting moved the approval of the committee's recommendation. Mr Towert seconded.

Mr. Smith's letters, from which we give the following excerpts were then read: -

About seven years ago he was led most seriously while in deep sorrow to ask," would God cast off forever and consign to eternal torment, upon any ground whatever, any of the souls which he had formed?" In the circumstances he had been brought to know there was nothing in God's word (he did not say the Scriptures) to justify the awful dogma of everlasting punishment. On the contrary it was the rankest growth of the mystery of iniquity which had succeeded to a marvellous degree in having its thoroughly malignant spirit ascribed to the hateful words put into the mouth of the eternal Friend and Saviour of mankind. Wherefore instead of being a truth of the gospel of God, it is the great and cruel lie which has been palmed upon and deceived the people of God. Hence it and all that pertains of it is Antichrist. He submitted therefore all creeds, catechisms and confessions being at best but human compilations; but when proceeding on such lines taking tares for truth, they were doubly and self-condemned, only tending to confirm in, rather than keep from, error.

Of course, he did not now attempt to prove but only to indicate the conclusions come to while searching in all sincerity for the truth of God as to the final destiny of their race. Some might be offended and ask what he had to do with this. Although he was only a missionary it became imperative to expose that which diametrically opposes the glorious Gospel in its divinest aspects. If seeking to eradicate from their popular theology the foulest blot that ever blighted any religion -eternal torture – were an offence, then he took the blame. True religion they could not expect to have while they remained so credulous as to allow any human formula to usurp the place of supreme authority in their Churches. These sources of error and confusion combined to render Christianity so equivocal in principle make it more than doubtful whether it would not ultimately prove to the world an unmitigated curse, rather than God's best and greatest blessing. What was the outcome of all the creeds suckled by the human element but to make the blessing the exception and the curse of the rule? Realising in some measure such a condition of things it would only be cowardly fear of personal consequences that would make him keep any longer silent. He then went on to state that he intends calling public attention to the matter by means of a series of discourses in which he will point out the fundamental errors of omission and commission in the Confession of Faith – for it could be shown to be erroneous on the cardinal points of creation, probation and salvation- and also how in the Scriptures the Divine word was to be discriminated from the human or the perfect truth of God separated from the tares sown in it by the enemy. So, the public could then judge whether he had or had not truth on his side.

The letter to Mr Gowans was dated the 24th inst. In it Mr Smith said that as he seemed by his suspension and the taking from him of his keys, to be cut off from all communication with the Board itself, he had been forced to address himself to one of its members. The letter proceeded.

"What have I done to deserve this treatment? The greatest immorality or crime would alone justify such hasty and extraordinary procedure. Only because I voluntarily and respectfully avowed to my belief in the everlasting Gospel of good tidings of good to all men and claiming the right to protest against that which not only renders it told in the highest and best designs but turns its best blessings into the direst curse. For this, and this alone, you are about to cast me out, without hearing one word even of explanation or defence. Gentlemen were I the vilest of mankind and you the most infallible, what more could you do? All I now ask at your hands, gentlemen, is to let me be tried before you utterly reprobate and condemn me. I feel for the difficult position in which you are placed. Great as it is, however, mine in various ways is much greater".

Mr Gowans then seconded Bailie Cranston's motion. He could not agree to dismiss Mr Smith in such a way. He had been Chaplain for 14 years and had discharged his duties very efficiently and he felt justified in saying that no member of the Board had reason to find fault with him. He had taken the responsibility of candidly stating his views and had seen it to be his duty to tell the Board that on the question of eternal punishment he did not agree with the Confession of Faith. During the past few years many theological questions and much discussion had agitated the Church and the world, and he thought that in the present instance it would be well before dismissing the chaplain to have an interview with him.

Mr Lewis said that the simple question the House Committee had to deal with was to consider their relations to the 500 poor people in Craiglockhart. They had a duty to discharge to those people who had no other means of grace but attendance on the ministrations of the chaplain. The Chaplain had brought it under their notice himself and he did not now believe in the truth he formerly believed in and that it would be his life's work to subvert his old belief, which he now characterised as a lie, – a dangerous pernicious abominable lie- and he came to them to ask whether they would condone that conviction and allow him to preach the new doctrine in place of the old one which he undertook to preach when he entered their service. Mr Lewis said further that he happened to hear the Chaplain on one occasion, and it appeared to him that the discourse was largely taken up with the controversial element. In his position, to substitute theological speculations for the simple preaching of the Gospel was not desirable. Besides Mr Smith's mind seemed bent on expounding, illustrating and enforcing his new ideas and calling the attention of the public to them in a series of discourses. He had to ask the Board to say where the Craiglockhart Poorhouse was the place for such an exhibition. He ventured to say that it was not. He thought on the whole it would be much better to have a man there who would have his attention more directed to such a text as *"this is life eternal".*

Councillor Tait- *"that is what he is doing".*

Mr Lewis- *"that you may believe in him the only true God and Jesus Christ whom he has sent* "and dwelling on the other *"thou shalt not surely die".*

Mr Towert said the 500 in Craiglockhart did not believe in the doctrine Mr Smith was preaching. The house officials were compelled to attend his services and they did not believe in it.

Mr Gowans- *"who told you that?"*

Mt Towert replied he knew perfectly well that they sat there and listened with abhorrence. Besides, this Board was not entitled to take the money of the ratepayers to retain Mr Smith when the large majority of the ratepayers did not believe his doctrines (*"hear, hear"* from Mr McKnight) It was foolish of Bailie Cranston to talk of Mr Smith sending people to Heaven. He could not do it – it was the Gospel.

Mr Young said he was not particularly displeased at the man for having relieved the minds of the poor people by telling them that there was not eternal punishment. At the same time, it had been stated by several members of the Committee they had been to hear Mr Smith's services and that he had spent his whole time on that debatable subject, and not only so, but had greatly prolonged his discourse that he had preached from 40 to 80 minutes, and he did not think any members of the Board would care to sit more than 20 minutes at a sermon.

He had no sympathy for Mr Smith because of this, and while he was anxious to relieve the poor from future punishment, he was so terribly anxious to inflict himself upon them at present. As one of the minority in the Committee who would say that they did not want Mr Smith to change his views, but if possible, to avoid preaching them.

Mr Gibson pointed out it would be difficult for any member of the Board to explain their own position on this question of eternal punishment. He went on the principle of thinking as little as possible on these things because he thought they went beyond human understanding.

Mr McGibbon supported Bailie Cranston's motion, as did Councillors Buchanan and McDougald, the former of whom remarked that the heavens would not fall although they met Mr Smith and talked to him in a kindly and Christian spirit.

Mr McKnight said Bailie Cranston's motion was a motion just for arrest of judgement. Mr Smith was very proud, he understood, of this extraordinary, ridiculous production. He did not attempt to prove his statements. They were just the series of ridiculous assertions without one proof. Would any man tell him that they paid Mr Smith to find out the truth of Scripture, and then having found it to preach it? Was ever such nonsense talked? The Board had made a contract with this man, a member of the Established Church and he had now made a change, and they were not to pay him for his change of views. He had broken the contract on which he retained his house and salary. He denied the canon; he denied the Scriptures, the Word of God (cries of "*no, no*") and he would just laugh at any committee they might appoint.

Bailie Cranston rose and declared that Mr Smith did in no such way deny the Word of God. He thought the man was really honest, although he might have committed an error in this. The way in which Mr McKnight had spoken was a spirit of pure despotism. It was a spirit of all law that a man had the justice done to him of hearing his condemnation. Mr McKnight, a lawyer, ought to have known better than to suppose that a man was ever condemned without being heard. This man should be heard, and they should see what could be done to save himself his wife and his family.

Mr McKnight asked Bailie Cranston to withdraw the word 'despotism', but he was unsupported, nobody taking any notice of the appeal. Councillor Tate withdrew his motion in favour of Bailie Cranston's.

A vote was then taken, when 14 voted for Bailie Cranston's motion, and 11 for the approval of the committee's report. It was then pointed out that according to the rules the committee must be the House Committee who, however, could appoint another committee to consider the subject. The meeting then terminated.

The Evening Telegraph April 1884
The ex-chaplain of Craiglockhart on his defence

Last night in the Waverley Hall Edinburgh, Mr. Smith, late chaplain of the Edinburgh City Poorhouse, began a course of lectures in which he means to define his views on eternal punishment for which quite recently he was dismissed from his chaplaincy. There was a fair attendance. Mr. Smith, who discoursed with a rather pleasant manner, chose for the basis of some remarks John III V 16 "God so loved the world etc". This, he said, was the greatest of Gospel truths and they ought to see that it was set free from all errors. If that were done, he thought there would be fewer sects and less scepticism. 20 years ago, he held the truth in the traditional form, but when he became a missionary and came into contact with the practical difficulties of life, he began to wonder if it can be true. He was of the opinion that few thoughtful men can go into the closes and lanes of their cities and see the young and the old die – people who had never had a chance in the world – without feeling that the traditional form of truth on this particular subject did not apply to them. He had to fall back upon the great Mercy of God. After some years as a missionary, he became a candidate for the chaplaincy of Craiglockhart and he framed his trial sermon so as to show that he would not be bound by the Confession of Faith[36], more especially by that part of it which declared that God had fore-ordained for all eternity that certain men and angels were doomed to destruction. It was a mistake, therefore, to say that he broke an engagement. Going on to speak on the general question, he said it was astonishing how little there was in the Bible to support the dogma of eternal punishment. The dogma of eternal punishment was a wicked libel on the God of grace and consolation; for what did it imply but this, that wickedness was to be perpetuated for ever? Such punishment was contrary to nature and absolutely opposed to the character of God, who was, as in the old days, "long suffering, merciful and gracious". Mr. Smith, who is possessed of a capital tenor voice, which he can use to good purpose, sang – for he said he sang the gospel at Craiglockhart as well as he preached it – in an effective way, Norman MacLeod's hymn "Trust in God and do the right "and "Comfort ye" and "Every Valley" from the "Messiah".

Dundee Courier January 1884
The Chaplaincy of Craiglockhart Poorhouse

The advertisement of the City Parochial Board for a chaplain for Craiglockhart Poorhouse in room of Mr Smith, who was dismissed for his views regarding eternal punishment, has drawn out a numerous and miscellaneous lot of candidates. The applicants number 43, the majority of whom are laymen, the list comprising 10 ministers, nine teachers, 12 missionaries, four or five small merchants, several divinity students, a gardener and a retired Major of the 74th Highlanders. The late chaplain Mr Smith is again a candidate and he supports his claim by a reference to his past 14 years' services in the Poorhouse. He goes on to say:

"during all these years my relations with the board were without a single jar but for those unfortunate letters which I now perceive it was highly inexpedient for me to trouble the board with and I deeply regret having

---

36   The Westminster Confession of Faith 1646, a systematic setting-out of Calvinistic theology

done so. With this unfeigned acknowledgement of my first offence, I hope, gentlemen, you will not now look upon it as an unpardonable one; while I solemnly promise, that if again appointed, only to preach and teach the simple Gospel truths, as the managers may deem most suitable for the poor people under their care. Gentlemen, in conclusion, permit me to say I have no alternative but to appeal to your Christian sympathy, as the interests of my young and numerous family will be sadly imperilled if I am deprived of all income and left without house or home. There is nothing left for me to do but to cast myself entirely on the clemency of the board, trusting you may look favourably upon my application".

A well-known local Permissive Bill lecturer was also in the field and prosecuted a vigorous canvass, but, acting on the advice of his friends on the Board, he withdrew from the contest.

The House Committee of Board met on Wednesday. A leet of three has been chosen. The salary is £130 a year with house coal and gas. The names of those on the short leet are the Reverend Donald Sutherland Free Church Kirkmichael, the Reverend Duncan McRae, Congregational Church Linlithgow and Reverend J H W Johnston Glenluce. The first mentioned applicant had the greatest number of votes. It was generally thought that it was incompetent for Mr Smith to apply. Three votes however fell to him.

Mr Smith's Petition Fails

Edinburgh Evening News September 1885

The Edinburgh Established Presbytery met. Mr Thomas Nicol, Tollbooth, the Moderator. The Presbytery sat in private to consider a petition by Mr HW Smith, late Chaplain of Craiglockhart Poorhouse. The petition, it was said, was of a very vague nature and we believe that none of the members exactly comprehended its import; but evidently Mr Smith wished the Presbytery to make some deliverances regarding his dismissal from the chaplaincy of Craiglockhart Poorhouse on account of the doctrinal opinions expressed by him while in the office. The Presbytery decided that the petition was incompetent as they had no jurisdiction or connexion whatever with the city parochial authorities.

Our hero is difficult to track after his dismissal and eviction, with his wife and eight children, from his accommodation in the Poorhouse. He resurfaces, however, with a splendid appearance in 1890 at the end of the 'No Popery Fiasco' in Holyrood Park. He died in 1907, aged 74 and was buried in Morningside Cemetery, where many of his flock at Craiglockhart Poorhouse were also buried. His death certificate records him as a 'Missionary'.

Jacob Primmer's Invasion of Edinburgh

Rev. Jacob Primmer, 1842-1914, was a Church of Scotland Minister. He was a colourful character, well known for opposing Popery and Irish nationalism, as well as 'the demon drink'. His activities included making a trip to Rome to *"to expose the nature, aims and plottings of the Papal Anti-Christian conspiracy."*

Edinburgh Evening News July 1890

The Rev. Jacob Primmer and Robert Thomson intend to invade Edinburgh on Sunday the 20th inst., and a correspondence has passed between Jacob and Chief Constable Henderson in regard to the matter. The Chief Constable says. "Your proposal to have a 'Protestant Demonstration' on the Calton Hill on Sunday evening is not in accordance with the practice and custom hitherto observed with regard to Calton Hill. No such meetings have ever been held there on Sundays and I do not see any reason why the long-established practice should now be altered".

In reply, The Rev Jacob informs the Chief Constable "that (D.V.) our meeting will be held in the Queen's Park (between Holyrood and the Pond) on Sabbath week, the 20th inst., at 5.30 pm".

The Tablet July 1890
Scottish No Popery fiasco
Mr Primmer's last demonstration

The event of the week in Edinburgh has been the "Great Protestant Meeting" in the Queens Park under the auspices of the Reverends

Jacob Primmer and Mr Thomson. The meeting, by no means a success, has been chronicled as graphically as man could desire by the *Scotsman*. We give as much as our space permits of that account.

The Protestant demonstration which the Reverend Jacob Primmer originally intended to hold on the Calton Hill came off in the afternoon in the Queens Park, and resulted in a scene of rowdyism, which was only quelled by the interference of the police with drawn batons. 5:30 o'clock was the hour fixed for the commencement of the proceedings, but as early as 4:30 a crowd had begun to gather on the hillside between Saint Margaret's Well and the loch, where a lorry was drawn up to serve the purpose of a pulpit. The Reverend Jacob Primmer himself superintended the rigging up of the temporary platform with a table and a form and the hoisting of a crimson flag bearing the device "Christ our King and Covenant" in large gold characters, while the Reverend Robert Thomson, who was also announced to take part in the proceedings of the demonstration to protest against the foisting of a liturgy or popish Mass Book and popish images on the Church of Scotland, was observed at some distance from the crowd, seated on one of the roadside benches conning over his speech under shelter of his umbrella .

As time passed the gathering quickly increased in proportions till about 15,000 or 20,000 people were assembled around the lorry, most of whom were apparently drawn thither merely from a feeling of curiosity to see the preacher of the Hill of Beith (*The location of a famous armed Covenanters' preaching meeting in 1670*). There was a strong Irish element in the gathering, a large percentage of the non-churchgoing community and very few people who appeared to have any sympathy with the proceedings. Shortly after five o'clock, several large parcels on the lorry were opened and were found to contain some thousands of pamphlets headed *"Revolution of the worship of the Church of Scotland and liturgy to be imposed"*. Under the guidance of the Reverend Jacob, a number of men who acted as his lieutenants preceded to distribute these pamphlets among the assemblage, while another contingent, each member of which was provided with a chair and a basin, took up positions around the outskirts of the crowd for the purpose of making the collection.

As soon as the people in the crowd had each obtained a copy of the pamphlet, they proceeded to burn them, and in a few minutes after the first match had been lighted, a couple of bonfires were burning merrily on the hillside and were being kept ablaze by numbers of children who ran about the crowd and gathered up the pamphlets from those who were too far off to reach the fire. The smoke was rising in two thin white wreaths when the Reverend Mr Primmer, accompanied by the Reverend Robert Thompson, whose meditations had been brought to an abrupt close by his colleagues' announcement that the time was nearly up, ascended the lorry and were greeted with an outburst of hooting, such as an unpopular political candidate might have expected from a meeting packed with supporters of his opponent. A few pieces of turf were thrown at the heads of the Reverend gentlemen but, though the portly form of the minister of Well Park offered an easy mark for these missiles, neither he nor his less robust companion appeared to be hit. Some of the people in the vicinity of the platform however were not so fortunate, and a few silk hats fared rather badly at the hands of the more demonstrative persons in the crowd. The hostile attitude of the assemblage seemed rather to disturb the equanimity of the occupants of the lorry and they took their seats on the form with some trepidation.

The Reverend Jacob Primmer gave out the Hundredth Psalm amid jeering and laughter, which continued while the verses were sung by a few people in the vicinity of the lorry. He next engaged in devotions, but the hubbub was so great that hardly a word could be heard, even by those who are only half a dozen yards off. A roar of laughter coming from the hillside as a well-directed piece of turf caught one of the occupants of the platform on the chest. Mr Primmer diverged from the subject on which he was giving special thanks to remark, "*oh Lord these poor men and women don't know Thee, or they wouldn't laugh*" which only served to create more merriment among those who caught the words.

The Reverend Mr Thompson then rose to read a portion from Scripture, but as he prefaced his reading with a threat to the effect that if the crowd would not keep quiet, he would make them, he met with a reception which was even more lively than that accorded to his colleague. He was so nervous that he omitted to announce the book from which he was reading, merely giving out the "18th chapter". Amid cries of *"speak out"* and *"shut up"*, he struggled on through a portion of the chapter, but ultimately came to an abrupt close by adding to the verse he happened to be reading *"and so forth "*and shouting at the top of his voice" *will you men of Edinburgh suffer the popish Irish to -..."* the end of the sentence was drowned in the roar which followed and the Reverend Mr Primmer, amid cries of *"Jacob again"*, gave out the 23rd Psalm. The gentleman who undertook the duties of precentor[37] got a few voices to join him, but the sound of the singing was drowned in catcalls, hooting and various other forms of interruption.

The Psalm being ended, the Reverend Mr Primmer launched into a discourse, little of which could be heard, for as soon as he directed his attack upon what he described as the Romanisers in the Church of Scotland, he was met with such an outburst of hisses from the Roman Catholic element, that his voice was completely drowned. He complained of the refusal he had received to be allowed to hold a meeting on the Calton Hill and added that though an attempt had been made to put him down, he was not the man to be put down. A member of the betting fraternity, who was standing near the lorry, on hearing this declaration in a few minutes a variety of prices were being offered in different parts of the ground, the popular offerings being however *"evens on Thomson"* and *"two to one on Jacob"*. Mr Primmer's address resolved itself into a warning that the laws of the church were being defied and that popery and prelacy set up once more.

The more the noise increased, the louder he shouted, but he could not make himself heard above the din. Mr Thomson, who been looking about anxiously for a few minutes, turned round to the people who were standing behind the platform and excitedly called someone to send half a dozen police to keep those Irish quiet. It was only he said a wheen[38] Irishmen that were making all the disturbance. Mr Primmer, during a minute of comparative quiet, was proceeding

---

37   Precentor- the person who leads the singing or prayers in a congregation.
38   Wheen- a few

to inform his hearers that he had been at St Giles that morning, when Mr Thomson provoked a renewal of the disturbance by shaking his head at the assemblage and exclaiming *"we will send for the police for you"*. Mr Primmer went on to denounce the sensational worship of the deity which he had seen that morning in St Giles and to express pity for the soldiers who sang praises there to the music of the fiddle and the drum. These remarks were received with cries of *"Bow Wow Wow"* and a few more fragments of turf, while Mr Thomson stood up and waved to a policeman to come to their assistance. Encouraging shouts of *"go on Jacob"* and *"three cheers for Jacob"* induced Mr Primmer to continue but finding that the gathering on the hillside was bent on obstruction, he wheeled round and addressed the portion of the assemblage which extended across the roadway. The change of front was seemingly not relished, and the Reverend gentleman was emphatically commanded to *"get down you heathen"* and recommended to *"hurry up"* but he informed the people he was now addressing that the crowd on the hillside were a lot of Irish and he was not going to address them further. He wanted to speak to the men of Edinburgh and to ask him if they were going to tolerate a liturgy. Are we, he asked pointing over his shoulder, going to hand our church over to a lot of these blackguards over there? Glad to find that the audience on the other side of the lorry were not so noisy as those on the other, he plunged into his subject with some spirit, regardless of the fact that very few people could make out a word he uttered, as the disturbance was going on quite as general as ever. They stood up he said for God's truth and the good old Church of Scotland.

"Go it old man" exclaimed a voice in the crowd and the uproar was renewed. The Reverend Mr Thompson, in his efforts to pacify the rowdies, nearly fell off the lorry, but regardless of his colleague's narrow escape, Mr Primmer continued to harangue the assemblage, declaring that the Church of Rome was trying to rear her head again in the land; he related an incident in which a Refractory Nun[39] had been drugged, but the uproar prevented the story being heard. He concluded by moving a long resolution condemnatory of popery,

---

39   During the French Revolution, the Church was reorganised into an institution within the French state. Priests who refused the oath to the state were known as Refractory priests.

graven images and a variety of other matters. Having taken a drink of water with much ceremony, bowing with mock politeness to the assemblage, Mr Thompson said that this was the greatest meeting he had ever addressed. There were only two or three hundred wild Irishmen and half a dozen policemen now keeping them very quiet. Turning for a moment to the object for which the demonstration had been called, he declared that they wanted men of talent in the Church; men who had religion in their hearts and not in a book for tuppence halfpenny per thousand. A great uproar at this point caused him to turn round and exclaim *"You Irishmen go to your Home Rule meetings. You have no business here. I am not a stranger here. I know these boys from the Cowgate"*. He concluded by asking to be excused from saying any more, as it was a difficult thing to speak with such an audience behind him who howled at him, instead of cheering him when he said a good thing.

As soon as Mr Thomson resumed his seat on the form, Mr Primmer jumped up and put the resolution to the audience, but little interest was taken in the show of hands, the attention of the assemblage being directed to a man who was observed scrambling onto the lorry with a paper in his hand. He turned out to be Mr William Smith, ex chaplain of the Craiglockhart Poorhouse, who announced that he had a counter motion to propose. His appearance was hailed with an outburst of cheers and hooting, but the occupants of the platform resented his intrusion and Mr Primmer endeavoured to push him off. These signs of hostilities on the platform delighted the crowd and the disturbance and uproar increased. Some more turf found its way onto the lorry towards which the crowd began to surge, evidently with the intention of storming it. While Mr Smith and Mr Primmer were engaged in a wordy strife on the platform, not a word of which could be heard even by those in the vicinity of the lorry, the Irish element began to look somewhat menacing. Mr Smith tried to mount the form, but the minister of Town Hill promptly pushed him off, telling him he had no business there. But Mr Smith was not easily to be dealt with. He took off his hat and began addressing the assemblage from one side of the lorry, while Mr Primmer pronounced the benediction on the other, but not a word on either side could be heard. Some of the Reverend gentleman's supporters, among whom was the precentor, came to the aid of Mr Primmer.

When the rowdy element in the crowd saw that hostilities had commenced on the platform their attitude at once became threatening. Just at that moment, Superintendent Bain, who was in charge of a strong detachment of police posted inconspicuously about the ground, ordered his men to the front. About a score or more constables with drawn batons, headed by Inspector Christie, charged through the crowd from different points and they laid about them with such effect, that in a couple or three minutes, the space around the lorry was cleared and Mr Smith was bundled off the platform. In charge of a couple of policemen and attended by a large following, he was marched out of the park. Meanwhile the Reverend Robert Thomson, being assisted down from the lorry, had made off as fast as his legs would carry him, leaving his colleague to face the storm alone. Mr Primmer, whose silk hat bore unmistakable traces of the fray, stuck to the platform while the police were forcing back the crowd and, in an excited state, explained to those around him that Mr Smith had no right to mount his platform, and ought to have desisted when called upon. The assemblage still remained jeering at the Reverend gentleman, but as the police formed a cordon around the lorry, no further hostile effort was made. Selecting the place where the crowd was thinnest, Mr Primmer shortly afterwards descended from the platform and hurried off, a dozen or two of his pamphlets being thrown at his head as he left the scene of the fiasco behind him. The gathering afterwards slowly dispersed.

Chapter 10
The Ultramontane[40] Miss Weir

The Misses Marion and Margaret Weir lived in Regent Terrace, still one of Edinburgh's best addresses. They founded the Abbeyhill Mission in the 1870s, ministering to a large working-class district around the nearby railway workshops. In their good works they were assisted by the Reverend Alexander Chinnery-Haldane, at that time Curate at All Saints Church Edinburgh (1869-1876) and who later became the Episcopalian Bishop of Argyll and The Isles. In 1881, Miss Marion Weir wrote, in the Scottish Guardian, an Episcopal weekly paper, "...it was rather the exception to the rule when we found steady church-goers and communicants of any denomination. The usual story was " We have got out of the way of going anywhere". A few of these have been gathered in; but what are these compared with the many that still remain without any religion and who even grudge the trouble of bringing their little ones to Holy Baptism?"

The Edinburgh Evening News May 1876
Alleged proselytism at the Poorhouse

The clerk of the Edinburgh City Parochial Board read a report of the subcommittee of the House Committee in reference to the alleged case of proselytism at Craiglockhart Poorhouse. It stated that the subcommittee, having examined the officials of the Poorhouse, Annie Scott and various other witnesses, begged to report that in their opinion the House Committee had in the matter of religious instruction not fully engaged to the rules laid down for their guidance. They found that Annie Scott was admitted to the Poorhouse is a member of the Established Church of Scotland. Prior to admission she had been taught the fundamental principles of Christianity and the Chaplain gave her weekly instruction in the

---
40 A person who advocates supreme Papal authority. Lit. a person who is situated beyond the Alps, representing the Catholic Church north of those mountains (16C)

ward in which she was placed. She could not tell whether she was baptised in infancy or not. She alleged that she did not wish to be baptised; and that when Miss Weir said, after having seen her once, that she would send a minister to baptise her, she understood she referred to the chaplain or a minister of the Church of Scotland. The subcommittee was further of opinion that though the proceedings adopted by Miss Weir might have been laudable in dealing with parties in their own dwellings, yet, in view of the rules of the Poorhouse and the responsibilities of the Board in regard to those placed under their care, they were of the opinion that she was guilty of an irregularity which might have led the Board into serious difficulty. The subcommittee would recommend that, with a view of avoiding any risk of this kind in future, the House Committee should strictly adhere to the rules laid down for guidance.

The Chairman said that he had received a letter from Miss Weir requesting a representative should be heard on her behalf before the Board came to a decision. He had promised to lay the request before the Board, and it was for them to say whether it should be granted. He believed there was a gentleman in attendance on Miss Weir's behalf.

Mr. Grant said he thought it would be very irregular to allow an outsider to discuss the question with the Board. Miss Weir had friends on the Board, whom he thought were quite competent to represent her. He moved that they should refuse to hear the gentleman who was in attendance. Mr. Steel felt it was a very reasonable proposal that the gentleman should be heard. Mr. Murray supported this view. The question involved very much the reputation of the Board. There had only had one side of the question and some thought the girl Scott had told her story very much as she was wanted to do. Mr. Hall suggested that the reports should be re committed to the subcommittee and that the gentleman who wished to appear for Miss Weir should be heard by them. Mr. Doig objected to opening such an abominable case for discussion in the Board. There had been quite enough of that already. Mr. Gowans took exception to Mr. Doig calling the case abominable. If the evidence of the witnesses were read to the Board, they would see the language was far too strong. He thought it quite competent for them to admit this gentleman who appeared for Miss Weir and to hear him. Mr. Lewis moved that they should recommit the report to the subcommittee with instructions to hear the gentleman who appeared for Miss Weir. Mr. Councillor Hall seconded the motion which after some discussion was agreed.

The North Briton January 1877

The special meeting of the City Parochial Board was held on Monday in order to give effect to the resolution in reference to Miss Weir's treat to the inmates at Craiglockhart Poorhouse. Mr. Hope the chairman not being present, some discussion took place as to who should take the chair.

The Inspector Mr. Grade read the notice calling the meeting and stated that the requisition in question was not included in it. Several members expressed surprise that they should be called consider a requisition and the requisition was not included in it. After much desultory conversation, it was moved the Board proceed no further into the matter into the meantime. It was also at moved that the Board proceed to business with reference to Miss Weir's proposed treat to the inmates of Craiglockhart Poorhouse. Mr. Doig moved the approval of the minutes in a long speech. Mr. Kinnear moved an amendment to the effect that the Board, finding that the House Committee had not carried out resolution and instructions given it on the 18th to allow Miss Weir to give a treat to the inmates at Craiglockhart for which she had applied, but on the contrary instructed the House Governor not to take any assistance from her and her friends, but to take only the assistance of the ordinary house officials, hereby direct the committee to allow Miss Weir and her friends to give a treat in the manner she had formerly done and to intimate the resolution to the House Governor.

In the course of the discussion, the requisition was handed in and read by the Chairman. Mr. Grant pointed out that the House Governor was not to blame in a matter. He produced a book which had been given as a present to the girl who was an inmate of the house. On the title page it was stated that the book was presented by Miss Weir with the hope that the girl might learn more and more the worth of prayer, which was all very good. There were some titles appended which the Mr. Grant could not make out.

Mr. Doig – *"Go on with your speech"*.

Mr. Grant, continuing, said he would read some of the principal prayers in the book (*"go on"* and *"no, no"*)

One began *"O Holy Virgin"* –

Mr. Doig – *"We don't want more. You have given us the title of the book, which is sufficient"*.

Mr. Grant said that the book was as rankly Roman Catholic as anything could be.

Mr. Kinnear – *"We have nothing to do with Roman Catholics".*

Mr. Grant said Miss Weir had got admission to the house as a Protestant, he asked if it were possible for a lady to teach, one moment Roman Catholicism and the next Protestantism. As well mind Dr. Begg[41] take Father Rigg's pulpit and preach Roman Catholic doctrines and vice versa. He contended that Miss Weir was not a fit person to give the inmates instruction. She had given him more trouble than all the paupers he had ever had to deal with.

A voice- *"You should pray for her, Mr. Grant "*(laughter)

Mr. Grant then produced a book given to another inmate, he said by Mr. – He would not call him 'Father' – Chinnery and read the inscription on its title page.

Mr. Doig- *"I object, Mr. Chairman, to any further prayers being read. We had enough of prayers yesterday"*

Mr. Grant, continuing, said that before going further, he would explain that the girl to whom this book was presented had applied for

---

41   The Very Rev Dr James Begg, a key figure in the Scottish Reformation Society

admission as a Presbyterian belonging to the Established Church. She had come in contact with Miss Weir lying on her bed.

Mr Doig – *"How could she do that?"* (Laughter)

Mr. Grant said that the girl had been asked if she were baptised, and she replied that she did not remember. He did not think that the Chairman or any of them would remember when they were baptised. Mr. Chinnery goes a day or two after without being requested, without the knowledge or consent even of the Governor and gets her baptised.

Mr. Doig- *"I rise to order".*

Mr. Chairman to Mr. Grant – *"Let us have none of your prayers here, Mr. Grant".*

Mr Grant – *"The prayers are none of mine".*

The Chairman – *"If Mr Doig objects to the prayers being read, I would take it as a personal favour if Mr Grant would be done as soon as possible"*

Mr. Grant said that what Mr. Chinnery then did was to write *"We receive this person in the name of the Cross."* The priest officiating then made his cross. Was that the way to treat a girl who had gone into the Poorhouse as belonging to the Presbyterian Church? A member asked if it were the form of religion Mr. Grant was ridiculing, and said if that was the case, he objected to him doing so.

Mr. Grant – *"I can show you a handful of cards when he has baptised right and left without any authority, and without the knowledge of the Governor or anybody else."*

After some remarks by other members the motion and amendment were put to the vote and was carried by a majority of one.

The Truth January 1877

The clearest illustration of these difficulties afforded by the case of Miss Weir which has for some time past been a cause célèbre in Scotland, where her wrongs have been discussed at great length by the public and the press. Stated concisely, her case is this: Miss Weir is a lady who some time ago obtained the *entrée* of the Craiglockhart Poorhouse, where she not only talked with the inmates on religious subjects, but provided them with "treats", especially at Christmas time: and in short did all that a kind-hearted gentlewoman could do to brighten the lives of the paupers. The managers of the Poorhouse aided and abetted her in kind and even gave treats themselves, till the religious elements in Miss Weir's ministrations induced discord between the authorities and the visitor. Miss Weir is an Episcopalian; nay more, a Ritualist[42], and she attends a Ritualistic church, in which a Mr Chinnery is the pastor. Miss Weir a gave a Roman Catholic prayer book to an Irish girl and Mr. Chinnery gave an Anglican prayer book to a Protestant girl. The managers however took it into their hands for that Miss Weir and Mr. Chinnery had jointly given the Roman Catholic book to the Protestant girl and when next Miss Weir asked leave to give a treat, she was denied permission to do so. Meanwhile the *Scotsman* supplies a moral to the unfinished story as follows:" the affair is conclusive as to the undesirability of allowing amateur missionaries into Poorhouses, no matter whether their mission is to bring treats or theology. They are not and ought not to be wanted; and they certainly infringe upon the principle upon which alone pauperism can be properly dealt with."

Edinburgh Evening News January 1877
The City Parochial Board and Miss Weir

At a meeting of the Edinburgh Parochial Board held this morning, another long discussion took place with a reference to the proposal of Miss Weir to give a treat to the inmates of Craiglockhart Poorhouse. Mr. Hopper the Chairman of the Board presided. From

---

[42] 'Ritualism' is an emphasis on the rituals and liturgical ceremony of the Church.

the minutes of the House Committee, it appeared that Mr. Kemp the Governor of the Poorhouse had asked for an explanation of the resolution of the Committee on their books and whether he was to accept the assistance of Miss Weir's friends in dispensing a treat. Dr. Ritchie moved, seconded by Mr. McEwan, that Mr. Kennett should accept the assistance of Miss Weir's friends.

The Chairman of the Committee thereupon stated that the business of the Committee was finished and that such a motion was irregular, as referring to a matter already disposed of by the Committee. When pressed however, Mr. Grant said he must move that the treat be given in same way as decided by the managers, this being what the Committee had already decided upon. The Chairman, after discussion, ruled that the motion was out of order and could not be put. Some discussion took place as to whether Mr. Kemp had received any instructions as to the treat ,beyond what had been given by the Committee, after which Mr. Kinnear moved: "*Seeing there is some dubiety as to the instructions given to the house governor in regard to the treat to be given to the inmates by Miss Weir, the Board authorise her to give a treat, instruct the house governor accordingly, the house governor to make all necessary arrangements with Miss Weir which he may consider expedient on the occasion*".

Mr. Councillor Mitchell said he visited the Poorhouse on Friday and the Governor informed him that if the treat was to take place just now, he would not be responsible for the discipline of the house. They should respect the opinion of the Governor in this matter. Mr. James said he had no doubt if the Board gave permission for the treat to be given, the Governor would be supported in maintaining order in the Poorhouse. Mr. Duncan said it was not so much Miss Weir's entertainment that was objected to, as to what they knew of her before and her proselytising. Cries of "*oh, oh*" and "*no, no*". The Chairman said Mr. Grant was going back on things already settled. Mr. Grant said if the Chairman ruled he was out of order, he would bow to his decision. Mr. Grant could not see why the Board of Supervision should approve of Miss Weir's treat and disapprove of the managers', unless for the reason that Miss Weir was a co-religionist of Mr. Walker of that Board (manifestations of disapprobation and cries of "*no, no*"). If they were to allow this entertainment the discipline of the house could be seriously injured. It had been injured already and the ratepayers would feel the effect. Since this treat had been announced, they admitted about 100 or more inmates to the house. ("*no no*") He would tell them something further, that since Miss Weir had commenced to visit the house four or five years ago, the inmates of her denomination had doubled. This would no doubt increase the rates which they laboured so much to reduce. He and those who fought on this matter with him had done the work of the House Committee, and they would not be put into a corner by the obstructive and ornamental members who never attended a meeting.

The Chairman objected to be called an obstructive member of the House Committee. They had altered their meetings to the evenings, and he could not attend. Mr. Grant said that was not true, for there had been no meeting any other time but in the evening for the last 15 years. The Chairman said he might have made a mistake with regard to the committee. If he had done so he was very sorry. ("*Hear, hear*") Mr. Gowans said he thought Mr. Grant should not turn on the Chairman as he had done. It was the weakest part of his case. Mr. Grant said he respected the Chairman as much as any of them, but if he accused him of underhand work, he thought he was entitled to tell ratepayers who did the work. Mr. Tait denied that the inmates of the Poorhouse had increased on account of Miss Weir's treat. If they had increased at all, it was on account of those Mr. Grant and his friends had proposed. ("*Hear hear*") At this stage Mr. Lewis objected to the motion being passed, as proper notice had not been given. Mr. Kinnear moved that the standing orders should be suspended to allow the motion to pass. Mr. Lewis moved the standing orders be not suspended. On a division 12 voted for the motion and 9 for the amendment. The motion was passed. A division was not taken on the original motion, which was also declared to be carried, Mr. Grant protesting on behalf of himself and those agreeing with him. The meeting then broke up, but after nearly all the members had left the room, it was discovered that it required a majority of three fourths of the meeting to suspend the standing orders. In this way into the matter rests in the meantime.

Edinburgh Evening News April 1876

An amusing little farce was rehearsed at the meeting of the Edinburgh Parochial Board yesterday. To call this the ordinary monthly meeting is surely doing it an injustice or else the strength of the company must be severely taxed in reaching the same level every month. "Priest and Proselyte" would be a good title for the entertainment. The chief characters were sustained by Messrs. Lewis and Grant, Councillor Buchanan, Miss Weir and a nameless but very terrible old woman. The first scene reveals an innocent girl, called Ann Scott, inhabiting Craiglockhart Poorhouse. This simple maiden is a member of the Established Church and no doubt is as ignorantly devout as the most zealous Presbyterian could wish. She is however "got at" by Miss Weir, lady visitor, and of proselytising tendencies. This dreaded woman belongs to All Saints Church and is therefore nominally an Episcopalian. Mr. Grant, that stern defender of Protestantism, remarks however that" to belong to the Brougham Street congregation is not a whit better than Roman Catholicism", The mind of Presbyterian Ann Scott is worked upon by the subtle machinations of Ultramontane Miss Weir. The latter intended to consign her young proselyte after having her baptised by "Father" Chinnery, to the care of the terrible old woman who has the reputation of being a fanatical Roman Catholic- so much so, that no one could be with her a fortnight without becoming as fanatically between the Roman Catholic as herself. But here the vigilance of Mr. James Lewis comes into play. His keen eye detects the Romish wiles which are inveigling the orthodox inmates of Craiglockhart. Miss Weir receives summary notice to darken the Poorhouse no more with her presence; the spiritual adviser is also sent to the right about; and Ann Scott is to be boarded out in the country-it is to be hoped in the family of a Free Church clergyman so that the bad effects of her late training may be at once counteracted.

**Rt Reverend James Robert Alexander Chinnery-Haldane 1842-1906
Anglican Bishop of Argyll and the Isles.**

In the winter the Rev Chinnery Haldane assisted at All Saints Church Edinburgh and in the summer he looked after St Bride's, Nether Lochaber and St John's, Ballachulish. Married to an Irish heiresss Anna Chinnery, whose name he took, he could work where the church could not afford a stipend. He was a fervent Anglo-Catholic, who founded the Bishop's House retreat on the island of Iona.

Chapter 11

Some Notable Events at the Poorhouse

Evening Telegraph March 1895
Fire at Craiglockhart Poorhouse

Considerable alarm was caused at Craiglockhart Poorhouse by a fire which broke out shortly before 1 o'clock this morning. The flames were observed by one of the nurses, showing themselves in the top flat of G section which is occupied mostly by women and children. The alarm being given, the brigade of the establishment were turned out. It was discovered that the chimney had taken fire and that the fire had been communicated to the joisting. By the time the fire staff came upon the scene the flames were coming through the roof to such an extent that they were seen by the County Constable who was patrolling his beat ¾ of a mile away. By the promptness with which the outbreak was dealt with however, the fire was soon mastered, and the danger was comparatively restricted. Of course, a good deal of damage was done by water, and partly on this account the considerable number of inmates had to be removed to other quarters for the night.

The Edinburgh Evening News 2nd January, 1877
New Year's Day at the Poorhouses

As usual the inmates of Craiglockhart Poorhouse received a New Year's Day treat yesterday. About 1:00 the 200 inmates assembled in the dining hall where they were supplied with soup, after which Mr. Duncan Grant Chairman of the House Committee in the name of the managers wished them a Happy New Year. Mr Grant expressed the great desire the managers had to see to the comfort of the inmates. For no doubt this was a life of monotony and they would feel lonely at times, but they had very much to be thankful for. They were living in a house in the finest locality and they had every comfort and indeed the managers even went beyond the statutory role in order to make them as comfortable as it was possible to be. There were 674 inmates in the Poorhouse, of whom 66 were lunatics. The hospital contains some 300 patients at present who of course form part of the total inmates. At Saint Cuthbert's Poorhouse about 300 inmates were brought together at 1.00 and the dining hall and served with dinner consisting of mutton pie and a large ration of plum pudding and a jug of beer. They were mostly old and frail old men and women, with a number of children, all however looking a picture of cleanliness, while an expression of quiet satisfaction seemed to rest on the faces of most. A number of the managers were present including Sir James Gardiner Chairman of the Board. After dinner a short religious service was held, conducted by Mr. Cumberland Hill the Chaplain. There are at present in the house 215 Males 236 females 38 boys and have 36 girls-in all 525.

Scotsman January 1914
Treat to the Craiglockhart Poorhouse inmates

With their customary generosity, Sir Oliver and Lady Riddell of Craiglockhart House, Slateford provided a treat for the inmates at Craiglockhart Poorhouse. The dietary relief for the day consisted of breakfast-coffee and bread and butter; dinner- steak pie and potatoes, plum pudding, apples and oranges, with sweets for the women and children and an ounce of tobacco for the smokers; and tea – tea and current loaf. Dinner was served in the hall, which was decorated for the occasion, at 1.00. Among the visitors present were Mr. Lees vice Chairman of the House Committee; Mr. James Gibson Chairman of the Parish Council and Mrs. Gibson; the Rev. Dr. Burns, Mr. Addison Smith, Major Huie, Vice Chairman of the Parish Council, Miss Greenlees, Miss Rose, Mr. Alexander Goodall and Mr. James Kidd, clerk to the Parish Council. After dinner Mr. Lees wished the inmates a happy and prosperous New Year. The Rev. Dr. Burns who next spoke suggested that the name of the institution should be changed to that of Craiglockhart Parish Council Home. The chairman of the Parish Council also wished the inmates the season's greetings and stated that they were very much indebted to Sir Oliver and Lady Riddell for the kindness in year after year providing a treat for the inmates there. On the call of Mr. Gibson, three hearty cheers were given for Sir Oliver and Lady Riddell. Major Huie in the course of some remarks referred to the better position of the inmates at the poorhouses in this country compared with that of the inmates of some other institutions in England. At this stage Miss Lees read a letter from Sir Oliver Riddell offering to all those who participated in the New Year's treat the best wishes of the season from Lady Riddell and himself. A concert organized by Mr. Norman Neil, comedian, was then given.

The Scotsman December 1917
Sir Oliver Riddell's Poorhouse Treat (or not)

A meeting of Edinburgh Parish Council was held yesterday – Major Huie presiding. The chairman made a reference to the death of another son of one of their members Mr. Galloway, the second he had lost in the war. The members of the Council he said had a good record of sons who had fallen in defence of King and country. For a quarter of a century, said the Chairman, Sir Oliver Riddell had given a treat to the inmates at Craiglockhart Poorhouse at each New Year, but Sir Oliver was of the opinion that, in view of the fact that many ratepayers found it very hard to make ends meet and found it difficult to get food, it would probably be out of place to continue their treat at this time. No matter said the Chairman what the price of food might be, their inmates at the Poorhouse had to be fed at the expense of the ratepayers. He consulted some other members of the Council on the subject, and the general opinion seemed to be that Sir Oliver's was a reasonable attitude. Therefore, Sir Oliver would not give a treat at the coming new year time.

The Merchants of Edinburgh Golf Club ask that in view of the unsettled conditions prevailing on account of the war and the consequent diminished revenue caused by the absence of a large number of members on military service, the lease of the golf course at Craiglockhart should be continued from year to year until the end of the war, instead of as before for a longer period. This was agreed to.

It was agreed that a war bonus of £5.00 be given to all the officials of the council in the Inspector's, Collector's and the Poorhouse departments, irrespective of their salaries.

Edinburgh Evening News May 1908
The poor to witness Procession.

At the monthly meeting of Edinburgh Parish Council last Monday, it was agreed to appoint a committee of five members to draw up an address from the Council for presentation to the King and Queen on the occasion of their visit to Edinburgh, and we understand that that committee have made all the necessary arrangements for the presentation which will be sent through Lord Balfour. They have also adopted a scheme of decorations for their chambers in Castle Terrace, along which the King will drive. The Craiglockhart Poorhouse is also to be decorated. The balconies of the chambers will be fitted up to accommodate the members of the council and their friends who will afterwards drive-in carriages to Craiglockhart Poorhouse by way of the Hydropathic, where they will again view the procession. The committee have also made arrangements for the accommodation of the children at Craiglockhart Poorhouse and Craigleith Poorhouse. The children will be given a prominent position opposite the Poorhouse.

The Courier July 1911
Aged veteran has a tragic end – An 'incidental' fatality.

The body of the aged veteran who on Thursday fell from a crag while watching the military pageant in the Kings Park to has been identified is that of Andrew Millar, who was an inmate of Craiglockhart Poorhouse. He was formerly a private in the Highland Light infantry. Beyond this incidental fatality, the Royal Visit, with its attendant crowds, has passed without mishap.

The Scotsman September 1917
Edinburgh Poorhouse Governor's Exemption

The case of Mr William Young, Governor of Craiglockhart Poorhouse again came before the Recruiting Appeal Court in the Sheriff Court Edinburgh yesterday, Mr RL Blackburn KC presiding.

Mr Young is 38 years of age, single and fit for general service. The Appeal Tribunal granted exemption on 1st July last in order that the Parish Council might make arrangements for a substitute for Mr Young. The Secretary for Scotland has intervened bringing before the Tribunal the fact that the Local Government Board were of the opinion that no suitable substitutes could be found and that the General Board of Control considered that the case should be re-heard. Mr DL Addison Smith for the Parish Council stated that the Parish Council had advertised for an interim Governor, offering £250 per annum with board and apartments. No applicants however had presented the necessary qualifications. The number of inmates at present under the charge of Mr Young was 1114 including inmates of Leith Poorhouse numbering 150, who had been transferred. There was a staff of 80. Mr Smail representing the Local Government Board said that the authority did not consider that any suitable substitute had been found. The great majority of the applicants were without previous institutional experience. All those of such experience had attained it largely at hydropathics and hospitals and in subordinate positions. In answer to the Chairman, Mr Smail stated that the Poorhouse was one of the five largest poor law institutions in Scotland and was crowded to the full. Mr AD Wood, on behalf of the General Board of Control, explained that a part of Craiglockhart Poorhouse had been certified for the treatment of mental defectives. A substitute for Mr Young would require to have such experience as would warrant the number in continuing the licence. The list of applicants was not a very promising one. Captain Crabbie, the military representative, suggested with reference to the application of a man discharged from the army on health grounds that the strain of running Craiglockhart Poorhouse would not be so great as that of a Sergeant in the Army Service Corps at Salonika. The court refused exemption. Mr Young to be called up on October 31st.

And finally, some crumbs from the table ...

The Scotsman April 1923
The wedding cake souvenirs for Edinburgh institutions.
(The wedding of the later King George VI and Queen Elizabeth, the Queen Mother)

After distributing the souvenirs of wedding cake to the 5000 children who were entertained in the Industrial Hall Edinburgh on Thursday, Councillor John Stark who was in charge of the arrangements found that he had 400 pieces of cake left over. Yesterday Councillor Stark dispatched these in parcels to the Edinburgh Royal Infirmary, the City Hospital in Colinton, Leith Hospital and the Craiglockhart Poorhouse for distribution amongst the inmates.

Chapter 12
Epilogue: The Poorhouse Poet

It seems fitting to conclude these tales of the Poorhouse with the adventures and words of one of the inmates, Peter Sinclair, the colourful Edinburgh Poorhouse Poet. Finally, his touching poem sums up the plight of many of the unfortunates who ended up in the Poorhouse.

The Shetland News February 1886
A Poor beggar – Peter Sinclair to the Front Again

On Friday at the Edinburgh Police Court, a middle-aged man, Peter Sinclair, was charged with having been found begging, the offence being aggravated by a conviction for a similar offence in June 1884. The accused, who pleaded guilty, was stated to have begged from passengers and to have been the worse for liquor at the time. Sinclair said he had never been sentenced by the presiding magistrate. It was a considerable time since he had been before the Court and if he got a chance that morning, he hoped it would act as a warning for the future. He was a poet. He had written many amusing pieces, but he had never written anything that would do anyone harm. He had never used his small talents for any evil purposes. It was subsequently stated that Sinclair had been in custody since Saturday and in respect of this he was allowed to go.

Commenting on the above, a Glasgow newspaper says *"We are always very sorry when any member of the poetic tribe, like Peter Sinclair of Edinburgh, is brought before a Bailie on a charge of begging, and our sorrow is deepened by the fact that one is born and anointed, while the other is only made and appointed. It cannot be too often reiterated that a poet is a person who draws his inspiration from above, for the unregenerate intellect has dared to say that he commonly finds his inspiration in the pint pot; that, in point of fact, he is by mature a combination of rogue, vagabond and beggar; and that, as a consequence, he has no fixed abode of residence or steady source of income. These are* the mean views of a wicked world regarding a race of men, who are as modest as they are useful, and as entertaining as they are truthful. How often shall we have to say that a poet is a man and a brother and that he cannot live by inspiration alone, but by every mouthful of bread that goes into his mouth? It is little wonder that men like Peter Sinclair are driven in the despair of hunger into evil ways.

"It seems that Peter, who is a middle-aged man, was taken up on Saturday for begging on the streets of the Scottish capital and is still a breach of a respectable law, though the offender be a breechless Highlander, a shoeless Lowlander or a shirtless Paddy. The offending poet was brought on Monday before the Court, when it was thrown into his poor unemployed teeth that he had been convicted of a similar offence in 1884. If true, that only amounts to this, that a poet may be hungry twice in three years and prefer to beg rather than steal. But begging is illegal and poor Peter pleaded guilty and couldn't help begging in court, though it was only for mercy. "I am a poet" he said, "and I have written many amusing pieces, but I have never written anything that would do any harm or bring the blush of shame to the cheek of modesty." Surely a worthy confession, and it is doubtful whether some of his greater contemporaries could say as much. This is a Christian land and Edinburgh is an extremely religious city; still in that sleekest of communities there is a market for wicked rhymes and, had Peter been less virtuous as a poet, he might have been eating roast peacock and drinking champagne, instead of shivering on the streets and soliciting a few pence to buy a scone and a drop of cheap beer. May not a man have an alcoholic odour and yet be virtuous? May not the police have made a mistake? Common liquors are not needed to set the poet's eye in a fine frenzy rolling. He drinks at fountains unknown to the common constable. Even police sergeants know nothing of Helicon[43] or the streams that pour the blushful Hippocrene[44] out of the green sides of Parnassus. We doubt whether the Chief Constable has any knowledge of the incontestable fact that in throes of poetic composition there is a sort of "divine drunkenness", which is perfectly harmless and does not call for police interference. Peter Sinclair may have been busy composing a new "amusing piece" or

---

43   In Greek mythology, the site of springs sacred to the Muses
44   The spring on Mt Helicon whose water was supposed to bring poetic inspiration when tasted.

an ode on temperance, when they thought he was intoxicated. It was no doubt the poetic spirit, acting powerfully upon the empty stomach of the poet, which created the condition that misled the Bobby who took him in charge. It is the fate of the true genius to be starved when living and only sometimes adored when dead, which is a kind of mixed consolation. Edinburgh may yet come to admire him as a man, which is far better than being buttered as a poet by uninspired and greasy citizens who are totally ignorant of the mysteries of Apollo and the art of lofty rhyme. Let him stick to his creed of poetic integrity, which he set forth so eloquently in the Police Court and always bear in mind that it is better to suffer, even to die, than to sell the smallest of talents for a bowl of porridge. The honest poet who is also sober and cleanly, howe'er so poor, is, if not king of men, at least a very superior person".

Edinburgh Evening News June 1902
Peter Sinclair Annoyed

At Edinburgh City Police Court today, Peter Sinclair, "poet" who was sent to the Royal Infirmary a week or two ago from the Court, made another appearance charged with creating a disturbance in George Street and Rose Street last night, shouting and uttering oaths and jostling against passengers. Sinclair pleaded guilty, explaining he was "much annoyed at some of those blackguards using bad language and he lost his temper". Having regard to his previous record, Bailie Gibson passed sentence of 60 days' imprisonment. Peter bowed, "I thought as much", he said, and expressing a pious wish as to the Bailie's future fate, he passed into the cells.

Edinburgh Evening News October 1902
Peter Sinclair in Cricketing Costume

Today's sitting of Edinburgh City Police Court was dragging out in a weary succession of uninteresting and technical cases, when the proceedings were enlivened by the appearance at the bar of the well-known, and on this occasion, oddly dressed, figure of Peter Sinclair "poet". Grotesquely attired in an elaborately braided white cricketing suit – a present from a leading Edinburgh doctor, Peter modestly explained – his hands encased in a pair of tan kid gloves and carting over his arm an overcoat, which he carefully deposited over the bar railing, Sinclair glanced round with a look of disappointment at the almost empty court room, produced an illustrated paper and a pencil and settled down to take copious notes of the evidence. The charge was that of creating a disturbance and collecting a crowd while drunk in Shrub Place on Tuesday, and the evidence bore it out, despite the long cross-examination of the poet, who on one occasion, attempted to draw from the constable a definition of the difference between excitement and drink. Bailie Murray quietly pointed out that the former was usually the effect of the latter, but Peter didn't seem to see it. When the case for the prosecution closed, Sinclair revealed his usual grievance. Two of the witnesses he had ordered to be cited had not appeared, but when called upon, it transpired, by court officers, neither of the gentlemen in question knew anything about either this case or the accused himself, so Peter had to content himself with his usual declaration of his intention to abstain from drink for evermore – providing, of course, he got away on this occasion. It was all in vain, however, for not only did Bailie Murray characterise him as a "nuisance to society" but sent him to prison for sixty days and put him under £5 caution for his future behaviour, with the option of another thirty days and expressed his deep regret that he couldn't make it more. Peter laughed, picked up his coat and strode out of the dock, expressing his devout intention of offering up prayers to save the Bailie from the judgement that would inevitably one day- and perhaps at an early day- be passed upon himself.

Edinburgh Evening News August 1899
A Prayer for the Bailie

Peter Sinclair "poet" 45 Gilmore Place, was charged with creating a disturbance in Princes Street last night, shouting and swearing, flourishing a stick and jostling and annoying passengers. Sinclair pleaded guilty in his usual eloquent manner, but impressively explained that he was going to London to see his friend to see "his friend Dr James Laidlaw Maxwell" and he would trouble the court no more if he got "one more chance". The prosecutor explained that the accused was drunk at the time, and when he was afterwards put in the cells, he broke six windows. The poet replied that the explanation of this was not of such a nature as to be fit for a public court.

Sentence of 30 days' imprisonment was passed, and this being just half his usual term, Sinclair cordially thanked the Bailie, and turning to the court as he departed, said he would pray for his lordship for his leniency.

Edinburgh Evening News June 1901
Peter Sinclair Poet and Gallant

Peter Sinclair "poet", resplendent in a new straw hat and a clean handkerchief, which he shook out daintily, amused the Court for half an hour. The charge was one of begging in Princes Street, and Peter's first complaint was that two young ladies in a tobacconist's shop in Princes Street, whom he had given orders to stand as witnesses for him, had not appeared. Sinclair, it transpired, had paid a visit to this shop and made himself so objectionable that a constable was called and he was nearly given in charge, but the ladies knew absolutely nothing about the begging and therefore had not appeared. Still dissatisfied, Peter demanded that the case be continued, and the girls brought to the court to give their statement, which might be different on oath. He knew them both very well, he explained, having often presented them copies of his poems and even bouquets of flowers. "Why, they often call me "the poet of Edinburgh" added Sinclair proudly. An adjournment was refused, and the case went to trial, when it appeared that, after coming out of the tobacconist's, Sinclair accosted several gentlemen and asked them for a penny. One of the constables added that the "poet" was drunk at the time. The Accused jumped up, "That's not in the charge; it is irrelevant". Peter's cross-examination as usual elicited considerable amusement. "Did you not take a 'tip' from a gentleman, who is an enemy of mine, to take me in charge?" he inquired of one of the constables, adding that he asked the question "*pro bono publico*" (Laughter). The charge of begging, it was stated, was the first of the kind against the accused and Bailie Telfer limited the sentence to one of 10 days' imprisonment, against which Peter howled a vigorous protest as he left the dock.

Edinburgh Evening News June 1901
Leith – Before Bailie Manclark
Peter Sinclair's Latest Story

Peter Sinclair "poet" made his first appearance at Leith Police Court this morning since 1893. He was charged with drunkenness and complained that the "statement was very much enlarged" but tendered a plea of guilty and five previous convictions were libelled. In extenuation Peter stated that he had come out of the Infirmary on Friday and went down to Portobello to enjoy himself. There he met several military officers and they had refreshments. His must have been drugged. One of the officers was very rude and said he was drunk. He treated the remark with silent contempt. On coming to Leith, he fell into the hands of a very humane constable. Peter was fined 10s with the option of seven days' imprisonment.

Fife Free Press and Kirkaldy Guardian July 1898
An irrepressible poet

In the beginning of the week, a highly imaginative individual, styling himself as Peter Sinclair, poet, created a disturbance in the town. In the forenoon of Sunday, he held forth at the U.P. Church door and sought to enter the building but was prevented. He turned up at the Free Church as the congregation was assembling at the afternoon diet and denounced them as hypocrites. Later on Sunday he made up to the Salvationists and declared to the Sergeant Major that his parents intended him to be a clergyman but found that there were too many rogues in the pulpit. Peter was again on the street Monday and Tuesday and was eventually run in for being abusive to a rival public orator. He was, however, dismissed with an admonition on promising to leave the town.

Edinburgh Evening News February 1893
Peter Sinclair Again

At Edinburgh Police Court today, Peter Sinclair, the poet, was placed at the bar having committed a breach of the peace and collected a crowd on Sunday at the foot of Leith Street. He pleaded not guilty and said "Sir, I would have had Mr Macdonald, the court solicitor but I find he is not in court and therefore I will conduct my own case". A constable stated that he created a disturbance at the foot of Leith Street by shouting and bawling and flourishing a huge stick. The accused said he was giving a sacred piece, which he had given previously in front of the Royal Hotel. Peter asked another constable if he called a recitation suitable for a Sunday shouting. This was followed up by his asking the constable if he ever heard a recitation given. Constable *"Not in your fashion"*. After evidence had been led, Peter asked that he might give a portion of the recitation to the magistrate. Bailie Gulland said they had no time for this, but Peter still persisted in his request. It was, ultimately agreed to adjourn the case in order to allow Peter to bring his witnesses.

Edinburgh Evening News November 1897
The "Poet" at the Police Court

Peter Sinclair, the "poet" who appeared at Portobello Police Court yesterday and whose case was continued, was brought up again today before Bailie Grieve, when he pleaded guilty to having committed a breach of the peace in Bath Street, and to maliciously breaking a pane of glass in the cell in which he was confined. Inspector Currie, the prosecutor, explained that Peter's misconduct arose though his having taken drink. The magistrate lectured the "poet" on the evils of intemperance and Peter responded by saying he was willing to take the pledge. A fine of 7s6d, with the option of three days' imprisonment, was imposed. At the close of the court proceedings, the court officials, wishing to test the honesty of Peter's intentions, asked him to sign the following: *"I promise by God's help to abstain from all intoxicating drinks as beverages and also to encourage others to do the same"*. Peter signed the pledge and left the courtroom.

Edinburgh Evening News January 1901
"Happy Days in Calton Jail"

Before Bailie Brown in Edinburgh City Police Court today, Peter Sinclair of "poet" and Police Court fame, was charged with creating a disturbance and breaking a pane of glass in a public house in Rose

Street. Peter, who, it appeared, had been in the prison hospital since the occurrence 14 days ago, was more than usually energetic in his protestations of intended reform. He proposed this time, he said, to turn over a new volume, not merely a new leaf, and to commence a new era with a new century. He spent a happy day in Calton Jail yesterday because he was sober. Bailie Brown: *"Don't you think it would be far better, then, to give you a few more happy days?"* (Laughter) Sinclair did not seem to think so and again protested that this would be really his last time. He would go away to Glasgow and never come back again. Bailie Brown *"But how long will you stop there?"* Sinclair *"I will stop till I come back in my carriage and pair"* (Laughter) Sentence of 60 days' imprisonment was passed, and Peter was hurried away, giving vent to his feelings in a manner which showed the "poet's" fine command of language.

Edinburgh Evening News September 1903
Portobello
Peter Sinclair at the Police Court

Peter Sinclair "Edinburgh Poet" re-appeared at Portobello Police Court today on a charge of drunk and disorderly conduct on the Promenade yesterday. He was attired in the garb of a soldier but had no boots. On his way to the court from the cells he recited one of his own poems about Portobello, which would probably be unappreciated by the constables. He welcomed back Bailie Grieve from his holidays and, on the charge being read, he replied that he was not guilty on this occasion. The bailie said that evidence would be led tomorrow, and the "poet" saluted in military fashion and was taken back to the cells.

Yorkshire Evening Post August 1898
The Poet in the Police Court

Mr Peter Sinclair, the Edinburgh poet, visited Dunfermline Police Court on Thursday. While waiting on the magistrate, the poet kindly recited his Jubilee Ode and his Address to Whisky. £1 or 14 days.

The Scotsman September 1897
A "Poet" in Edinburgh Police Court

Peter Sinclair, the "poet" made his reappearance in Edinburgh Police Court yesterday, charged with having about one o'clock yesterday morning made a disturbance by shouting and using bad language. He had been lying helplessly drunk at the gate of the prison and when a policeman roused him up, he started to make a great noise. It is some years since Sinclair was in the Police Court last, for he has of late been perforce sheltering within the walls of the Royal Asylum, which he quitted only on Wednesday. He was, prior to that, a constant attender at the bar of the Court and there was something pathetic in his laying down at the entrance to that "Christie's Hotel"[45] which he has endeavoured to immortalise in verse. The poet made an imposing figure as he stepped into the bar, his head, with the white hair and beard, held proudly aloft, while in his left hand he tightly grasped a roll of manuscript and in the right his hat. He bowed profoundly to Sheriff Sym, beaming around the while until his eye rested upon Sir Henry Littlejohn, who sat just within the bar and upon the worthy doctor's face the poet's gaze lovingly lingered. The Sheriff asked Sinclair if he was guilty of making a disturbance in Regent Road this morning. *"Yes"* replied Sinclair *"but I would like to explain in a few words* – "" *Well, just one word"* said the Sheriff *"I could not do it in one word"* answered the poet. *"What excuse have you to offer for being drunk and making a disturbance?"* *"I am not going to offer any excuse: but I wish to say that Sir Henry has given me an idea which cannot be bought with money and I am going to dedicate a new piece to Sir Henry; it will not be doggerel".* (Laughter)" *Is that all you have to say?"* asked the Sheriff. *"Yes, my Lord; you can do with me as you like now." "You must pay a fine of 7s 6d or go two days to prison" "Thank you, my Lord"* said Sinclair, with a graceful bow, and as he was entering the door leading to the cells, he turned round with the remark *"I will send you that piece, Sir Henry"* (Laughter)

---

45 Captain J E Christie Governor of Calton Jail 1876-1878

Edinburgh Evening News March 1892
Poet Sent to the Poorhouse

Peter Sinclair, the vagrant "Poet", who was a few days ago certified to be of weak intellect and was sent to the parish authorities, again appeared at the bar of the Edinburgh City Police Court on a charge of behaving in a disorderly manner in Rose Street yesterday. Dr H. Littlejohn again stated that the accused was still in the same condition and unable to plead. He was, as before, remitted to the care of the parish authorities. As the accused left the bar, he said, "*Well, my Lord, I am not deserving of your leniency at all*". Peter presented a very dejected appearance. He had no coat on, and he had his shirt sleeves rolled up.

Edinburgh Evening News July 1898
An Edinburgh Poorhouse Poet

Periodically Edinburgh cultivates or draws hither individuals of poetic bent, specimens of whose verse are spread amongst the community by itinerant means or otherwise to either harass or amuse, in whichever respect they are regarded. For three or four years past, there has been some competition amongst these poetasters for the local laureateship. There was Osborne Blackburn, prominent in his day; McGonagall, who "warbled of the beautiful"; Robert Paul, the "Aberdeen Loonie"; and Peter Sinclair, whose compositions generally got their best audience when he appeared in the Police Court, fortified with some rhymes dedicated to the presiding magistrate or Sir Henry Littlejohn. This little coterie waged a poetic war to the knife; it was the survival of the fittest. Blackburn is dead, Paul is unheard of and McGonagall has faded. But, though left practically unchallenged, Peter has come on evil days. If previously he shared with Paul the stigma of having appeared in the Police Court, any charity he partook of at the hands of the authorities was compulsory. But through lack of appreciation on the part of a listless public and too frequent recourse to a certain kind of inspiration, Peter felt the pinch of poverty so that, latterly, he has been forced to accept Government hospitality in another form and for some time has been vegetating in Craiglockhart Poorhouse. There he may be said to cease from troubling, and Sir Henry Littlejohn is at rest. But Sinclair was always too ardent a disciple of the Muse to forego its pleasures, and from his suburban retreat fragments of his art have reached the outside world from time to time. Even on poorhouse fare his genius seems to flourish. It appears that at Craiglockhart he has come in contact with those types that help so much as to make such institutions necessary- the drunkard, the gambler, the spendthrift etc. Peter is too true a poet to let such an inspiring opportunity slip, and the result is a creation entitled "Don't Fret", eight stanzas in length. The air is said to be that of "Rory O'More". Hearken to his muse:

Don't Fret

How foolish you are to fret over the past,
And for a slight error your prospects to blast.
Take courage, go forward, in future do well,
Let past folly now act as a warning bell.

The gambler, so greedy, complains of bad luck.
But to stop ere it turned he hadn't the pluck.
Then let him abandon this horrible vice,
Loss of peace and content is its terrible price.

The drunkard has lost all the charms of this life,
Morose, discontented, he's often at strife.
But let him take heart, keep the bottle at bay,
For where there's a will there is always a way.

The bankrupt regrets having had all those shares,
And great's his distress at cold poverty's cares.
But he must not give in, success is but gilt,
And crying's no use over milk that is spilt.

The want of success we often can trace,
To useless endeavours to be first in the race.
Then let us be careful not to pamper grim greed,
For the greater the hurry the less is the speed.

But with kindred ties to gladden your life,
A neat little home where there is no strife,
With God for your guide your troubles are gain,
For the sun seems brighter just after rain.

Appendix 1

The Burning of the Ship 'Kent'

By William Topaz McGonagall

Good people of high and low degree,
I pray ye all to list to me,
And I'll relate a harrowing tale of the sea
Concerning the burning of the ship "Kent" in the Bay of Biscay,
Which is the most appalling tale of the present century.

She carried a crew, including officers, of 148 men,
And twenty lady passengers along with them;
Besides 344 men of the 31st Regiment,
And twenty officers with them, all seemingly content.

Also the soldiers' wives, which numbered forty-three,
And sixty-six children, a most beautiful sight to see;
And in the year of 1825, and on the 19th of February,
The ship "Kent" sailed from the Downs right speedily,
While the passengers' hearts felt light with glee.

And the beautiful ship proceeded on her way to Bengal,
While the passengers were cheerful one and all;
And the sun shone out in brilliant array,
And on the evening of the 28th they entered the Bay of Biscay.

But a gale from the south-west sprang up that night,
Which filled the passengers' hearts with fright;
And it continued to increase in violence as the night wore on,
Whilst the lady passengers looked very woe-begone.

Part of the cargo in the hold consisted of shot and shell,
And the vessel rolled heavily as the big billows rose and fell;
Then two sailors descended the fore hold carrying a light,
To see if all below was safe and right.

*And they discovered a spirit cask and the contents oozing rapidly,
And the man with the light stooped to examine it immediately;
And in doing so he dropped the lamp while in a state of amaze,
And, oh horror! in a minute the fore hold was in a blaze.*

*It was two o'clock in the morning when the accident took place,
And, alas! horror and fear was depicted in each face;
And the sailors tried hard to extinguish the flame,
But, oh Heaven! all their exertions proved in vain.*

*The inflammable matter rendered their efforts of no avail,
And the brave sailors with over-exertion looked very pale;
And for hours in the darkness they tried to check the fire,
But the flames still mounted higher and higher.*

*But Captain Cobb resolved on a last desperate experiment
Because he saw the ship was doomed, and he felt discontent;
Then he raised the alarm that the ship was on fire,
Then the passengers quickly from their beds did retire.*

*And women and children rushed to the deck in wild despair,
And, paralysed with terror, many women tore their hair;
And some prayed to God for help, and wildly did screech,
But, alas! poor souls, help was not within their reach.*

*Still the gale blew hard, and the waves ran mountains high,
While men, women, and children bitterly did cry
To God to save them from the merciless fire;
But the flames rose higher and higher.*

The Burning of the Ship 'Kent'

And when the passengers had lost all hope, and in great dismay,
The look-out man shouted, "Ho! a sail coming this way";
Then every heart felt light and gay,
And signals of distress were hoisted without delay.

Then the vessel came to their rescue, commanded by Captain Cook,
And he gazed upon the burning ship with a pitiful look;
She proved to be the brig "Cambria," bound for Vera Cruz,
Then the captain cried, "Men, save all ye can, there's no time to lose."

Then the sailors of the "Cambria" wrought with might and main,
While the sea spray fell on them like heavy rain;
First the women and children were transferred from the "Kent"
By boats, ropes, and tackle without a single accident.

But, alas! the fire had reached the powder magazine,
Then followed an explosion, oh! what a fearful scene;
But the explosion was witnessed by Captain Babby of the ship "Carline,"
Who most fortunately arrived in the nick of time.

And fourteen additional human beings were saved from the "Kent,"
And they thanked Captain Babby and God, who to them succour sent,
And had saved them from being burnt, and drowned in the briny deep;
And they felt so overjoyed that some of them did weep;
And in the first port in England they landed without delay,
And when their feet touched English soil their hearts felt gay.

List of Illustrations

ii	A MacDonald
4	Creative Commons
15	Public Domain
16	Creative Commons
21	Creative Commons
31, 33, 58	By kind permission of Edinburgh City Archive
32, 34	A MacDonald
Front cover, 42, 51, 53, 54, 60, 61, 65, 71, 73, 81, 86, 90, 95, 115, 120, 126	A MacDonald from original pre-1897 photographs Edinburgh City Archive
44	Newspaper image ©The British Library Board. All rights reserved. With thanks to the British Newspaper Archive (www.britishnewspaperarchive.co.uk)
88	Private Collections. With thanks to Martin Callearts at www.aagordon.be and Neill Gilhooley www.neillgilhooley.com author of "A *History of the 9th (Highlanders) Royal Scots, the Dandy Ninth*"
109	A MacDonald from "The Wreck of the Kent" The Religious Tract Society 1886
150	A MacDonald
184	Creative Commons
Back cover	A MacDonald